A Beader's Refe

Jane Davis

Published by

700 East State Street • Iola, WI 54990-0001
715-445-2214 • 888-457-2873
www.krause.com

Please call or write for our free catalog of publications. Our toll-free number to
place an order or obtain a free catalog is (800) 258-0929.

Library of Congress Catalog Number: 2003108446
ISBN: 0-87349-554-3

Edited by Maria L. Turner
Designed by Marilyn McGrane

Dedication

I dedicate this book to Carole Tripp. You have been a mentor, teacher, inspiration, and most of all, a very good friend throughout my journey in beadwork.

Acknowledgments

Many thanks to my wonderful, talented editor, Maria Turner, who pulled this book together. As always, it has been a pleasure working with you.

Thank you Marilyn McGrane for creating the beautiful design and layout of the book.

Thank you Amy Tincher-Durik for getting this book under way. You have been a great advocate for me and my ideas at Krause.

Thank you to Carole Tripp of Creative Castle for your help in choosing and finding beads for many of the pieces on these pages and for coordinating many of the gallery items throughout the book.

Thank you to the imaginative and beautiful contributions of the gallery artists, who have allowed me to include their work in this book. The work of Delinda Vannebrightyn Amura, Margo C. Field, Kathy Henjyoji, Corinne Loomer, Lisa Taylor, Carole Tripp, and Liz Smith has enhanced these pages.

Thank you to Susan Lazear, owner of Cochinelle, and designer of the program I used for many of the charts in this book, Stitch Painter. This has been a wonderful program to use for designing and editing designs. Your support staff has helped me through every question on using the program, and I have found the program to be ideal for designing.

Table of Contents

Section 5: Projects 104

Introduction

After being shuffled around as a small category in either jewelry or needlework for years, beading has finally come into its own as a separate creative art and craft form. There are books aplenty on every type of beadwork imaginable, and bead shows and bead stores are everywhere.

With this blossoming of beading interest comes a need for more designs and more ideas on new ways to work with beads and create unique works. That is why I have created this source of designs and ideas especially for beaders. From the large centerpiece designs, to the small repeats, to the finishing touches of fringes and edgings, you'll find the components you need to create many new and exciting beadwork projects. And you have a variety of beadwork techniques to choose from, including peyote, brick, loomwork, square stitch, crochet cords, herringbone, and netting.

Following the charts and designs are a dozen projects showing just some of the ways you can pick and choose elements from the book to gather together a finished piece. Throughout the book, you will also find examples of inspirational pieces by various beadwork artists showing similar ideas and variations of patterns in the book.

How to use this book

I have envisioned this book from the beginning as a type of reference book, like a dictionary or encyclopedia, where you can look up an image by category or by bead stitch, or just thumb through it to get ideas for your next project. Therefore, I have numbered all the illustrations, and set up two indexes: one grouped by subject and one by bead stitch. There is also a third general index.

The photos of finished projects and the 12 step-by-step projects at the back of the book are meant to inspire you with possibilities you may not have thought of before. The rest of the book serves as a tool for you to use to make your very own special creations. I hope you find this book a basic resource in your beadwork adventure.

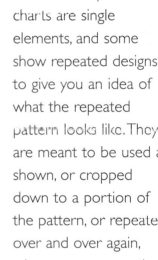

A note about pattern repeats

Some of the pattern charts are single elements, and some show repeated designs to give you an idea of what the repeated pattern looks like. They are meant to be used as shown, or cropped down to a portion of the pattern, or repeated over and over again, wherever your creative impulses lead you.

Section 1

Basic Stitches and the Graphs

The following stitches describe only the very basics of each stitch and are just meant as a visual aid in identifying the graph, not as an instruction for working the stitch. For more detailed instructions on techniques, such as beginning and ending specific stitches or turning corners, consult a technique book on the stitch. This book is meant as a companion book to my previous beading book, "The Complete Guide To Beading Techniques" (Krause Publications, 2001). You can find details of working the stitches there.

The graphs throughout this book are created for the following stitches. Because of space constraints and the evolving nature of beading, I was not able to include graphs for every beading stitch, so I chose graphs that are the most versatile, the most common, and a few graphs of stitches that I like because they are quick and easy to stitch.

Brick (Comanche) and Peyote (Gourd) Stitches: The same graph is used for both of these stitches. The peyote stitch is worked from top to bottom or bottom to top. Turned sideways, the graph becomes the reference for the brick stitch. I oriented most of the designs for peyote stitch since it is the more commonly used stitch of the two. It is also a faster stitch to work.

When using the graphs for peyote stitch projects, especially when you have cropped the design, be sure to check that you have the corner bead on the first row. In some cases, you may need to begin working from the bottom up to achieve this.

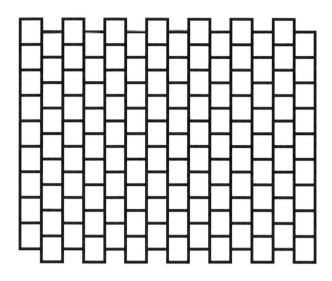

Herringbone Stitch: You can use the loomwork graphs for herringbone stitch, but they don't really show an accurate image of the horizontal stretch of the design. They also don't show which two beads to pick up for each stitch. The graphs in this section more accurately show the stitch structure.

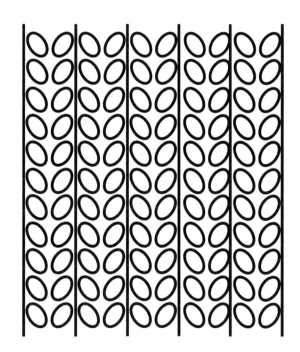

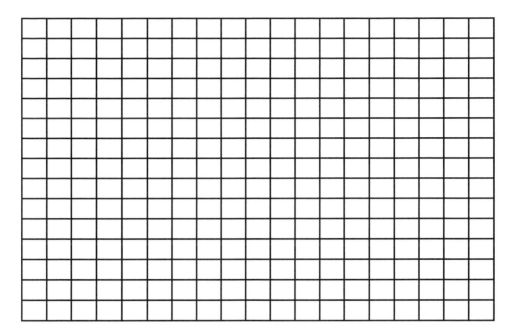

Loomwork, Square Stitch, Needlepoint, and Cross Stitch: This is a very versatile graph. Since it is on a standard grid pattern, it can be used for any project that uses a standard graph, from needlepoint to cross stitch to the bead stitches mentioned previously. I have set up the graph for beads on a loom, working most patterns from side to side.

The graph proportions differ from chart to chart, so be sure to calculate your finished size by making a small sample in your choice of beadwork technique. You can also get an idea of the finished piece by photocopying the pattern and adjusting the height on the copy. An example of the difference in the stretch of the graph designs is shown on the Black Victorian Gate Purse (page 148) and the cover design. The cover was made in loomwork, and the purse was made in herringbone stitch. The purse design is stretched a little horizontally compared to the cover loomwork, yet they both work well as designs.

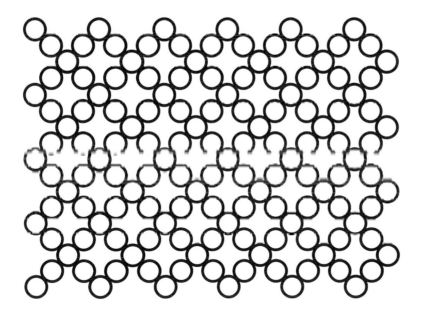

Netting: I chose a three-bead netting graph for the designs in this book. It is one of the densest of the netting stitches, which allows for more detailed designs than most other netting patterns. Netting easily lends itself to Celtic knotwork, so that is what I concentrated on for the designs in this stitch.

Section 2
Charts

Here is a collection of many pattern ideas, from small, simple repeats to large landscapes. You can use these designs in a variety of ways. The first and most basic is to just stitch the design as presented, making a flat piece of beadwork to use however you want, from placing in a tray or the top of a box to framing it for a picture. But don't stop there.

Most of the designs can be repeated to create a border. Many can be worked in one direction, then reversed and worked the other way, creating a mirror image of the design. Larger designs can be cropped and used just for small sections that create a nice composition for your project.

The charts are numbered and organized by stitch, with the stitch type at the front of the number. For instance, the second chart in the herringbone section is #H02. This way, you can easily find the chart you want to use in the stitch type you are looking for.

Brick and Peyote Stitches

B01

B02

B03

B04

B05

B06

B07

B08

B09

B10

B11

B12

B13

B14

B15

B16

B17

B18

B19

B20

B21

B22

B23

B24

B25

B26

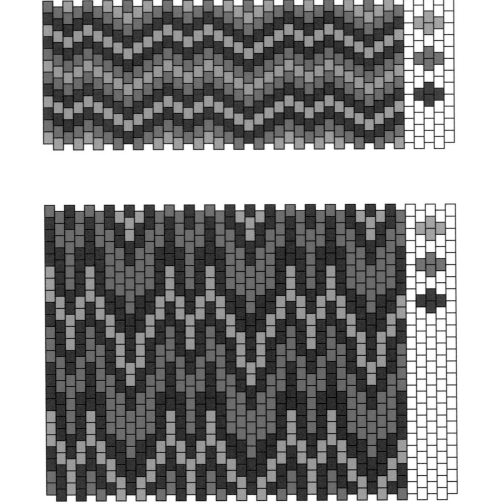

B27

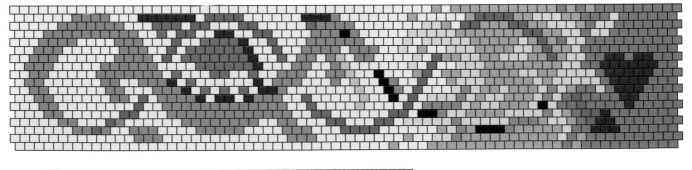

B28

B29

B30

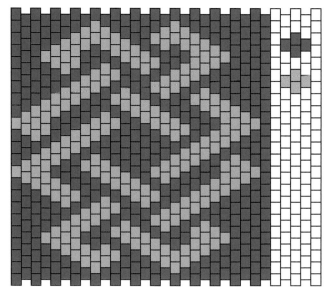

B31

B32

B33

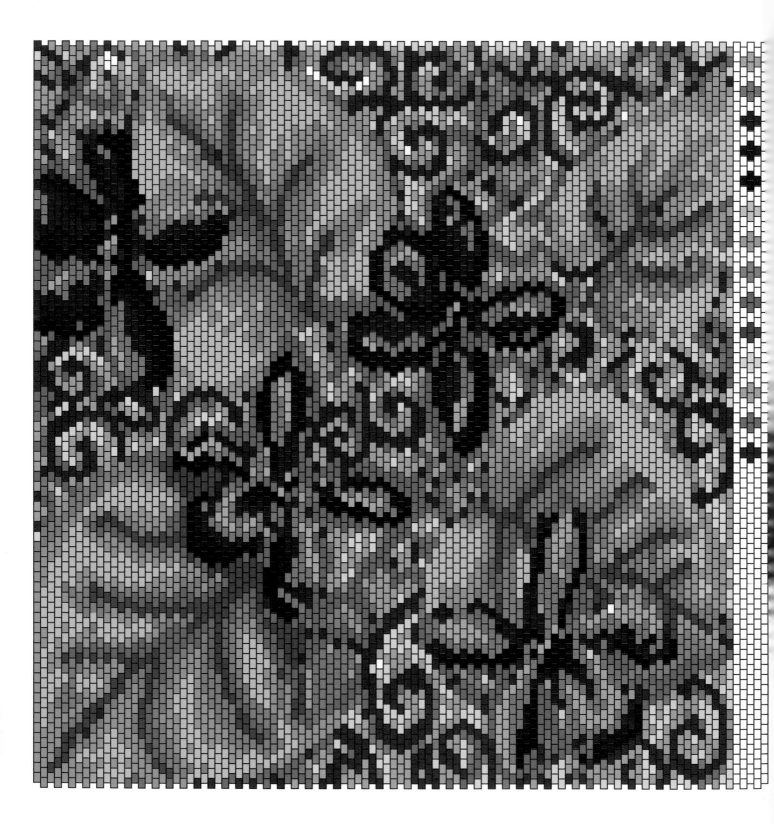

B35

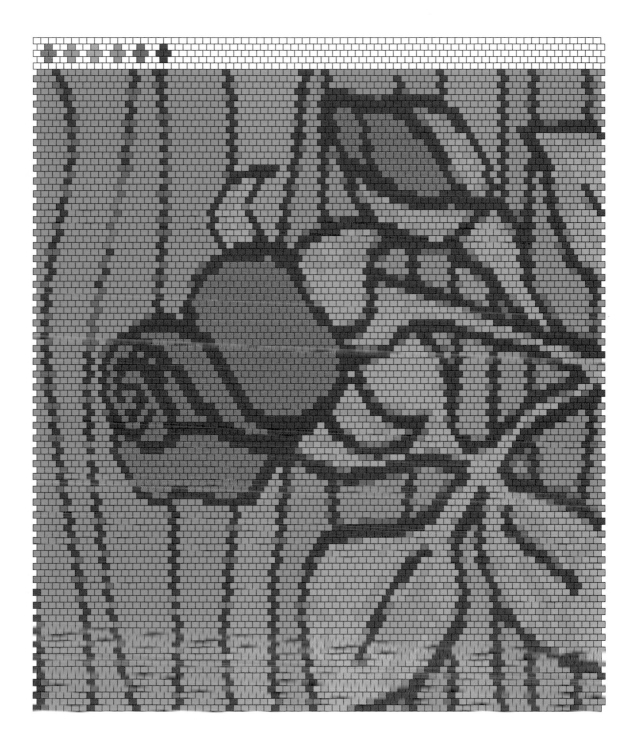

B37

| Brick and Peyote Stitches

B39

B41

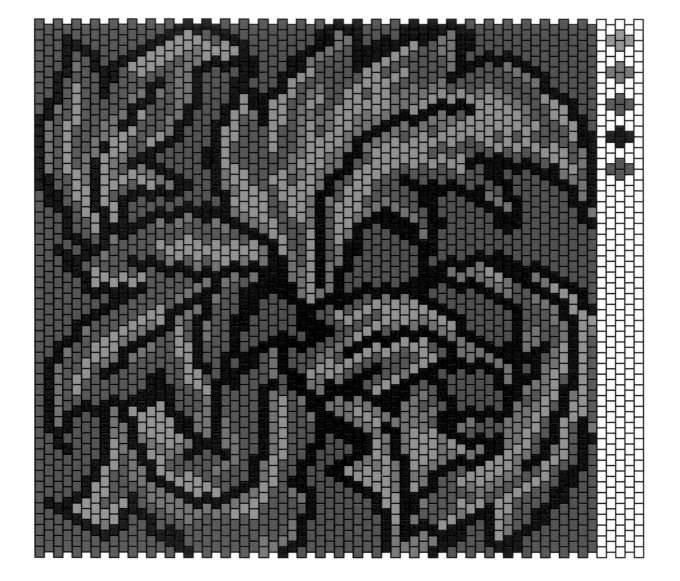

Herringbone Stitch

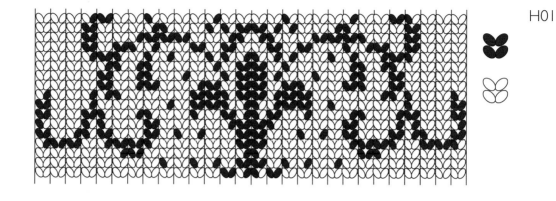

H01

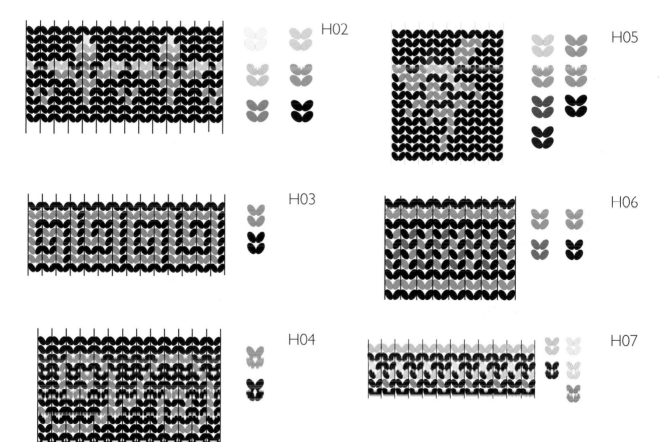

H02

H03

H04

H05

H06

H07

H08

H09

H10

H11

H12

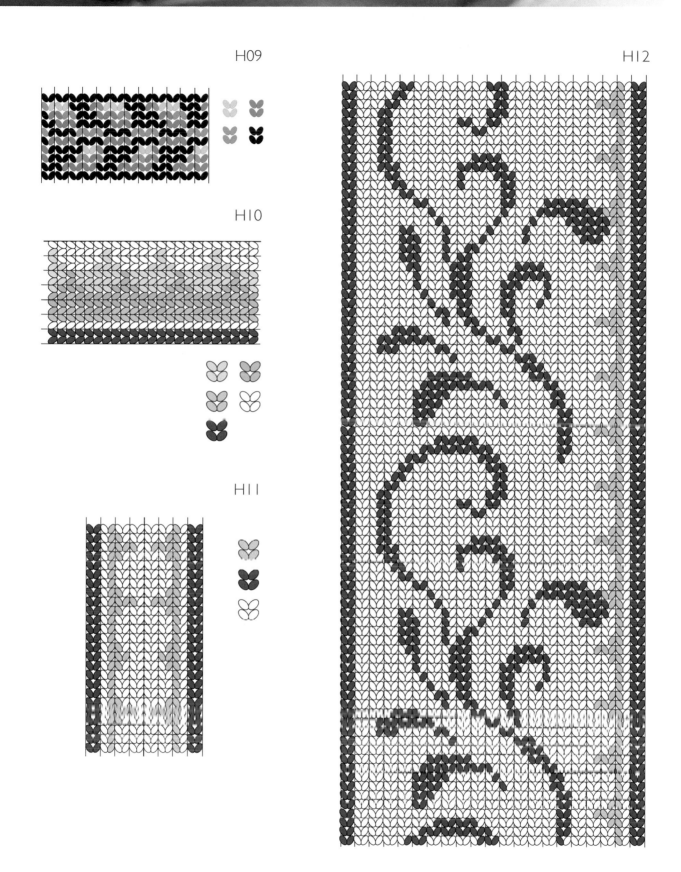

H13

H14

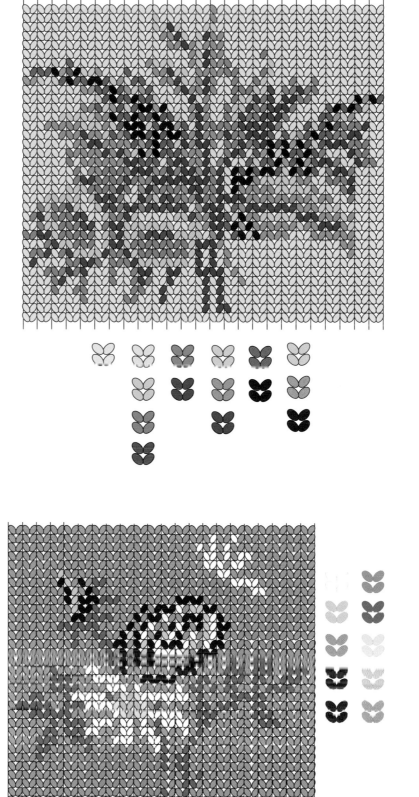

H15

H16

H17

H18

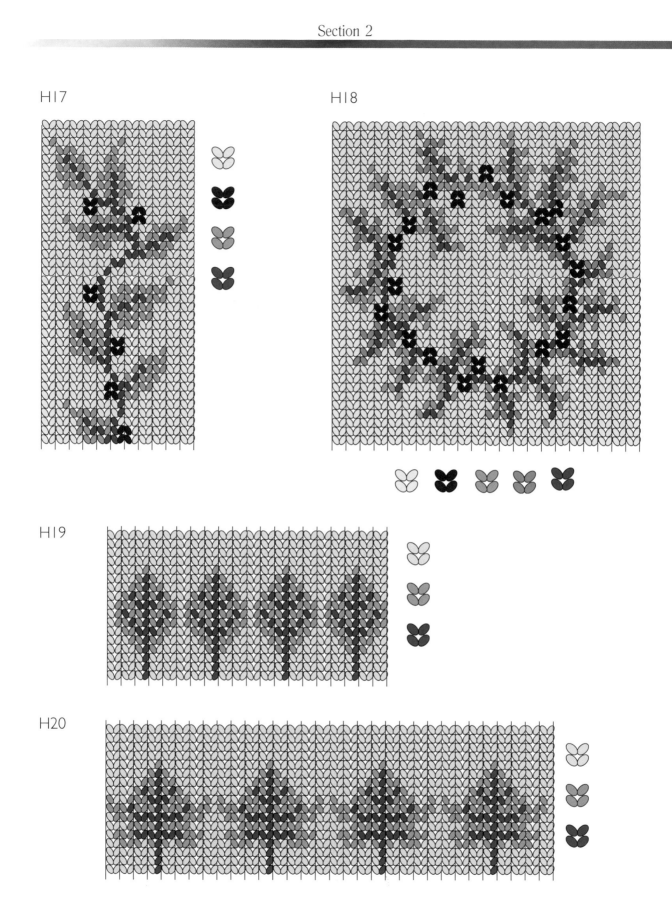

H19

H20

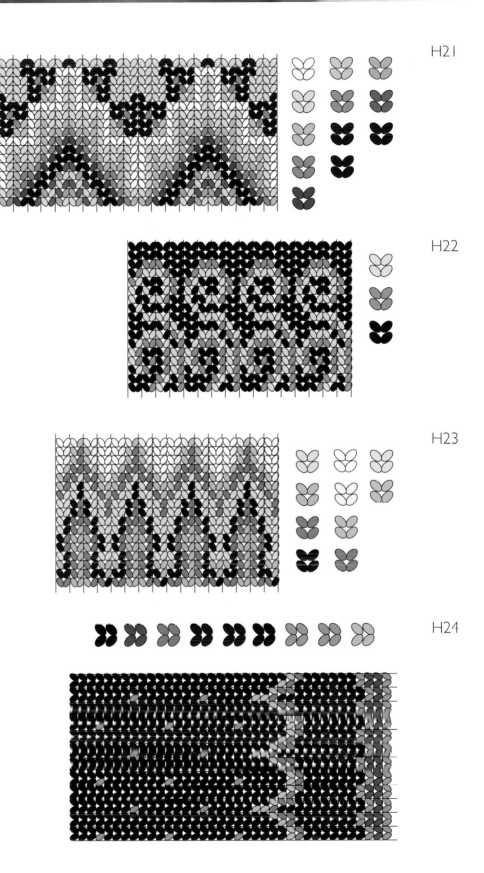

H21

H22

H23

H24

H25

H26

H27

Loom and Square Stitches

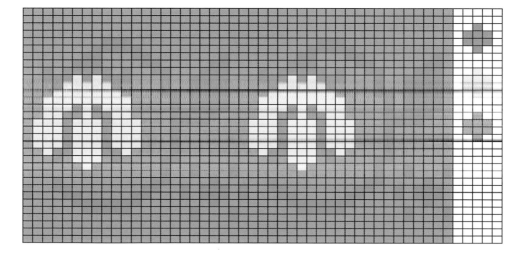

L01

L02

L03

L04

L05

L06

L07

L08

L09

LI0

LII

LI2

LI3

LI4

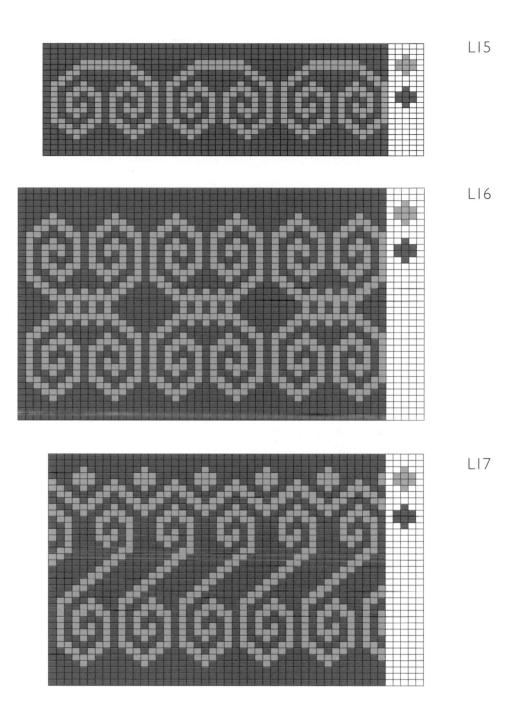

L15

L16

L17

L18

L19

L20

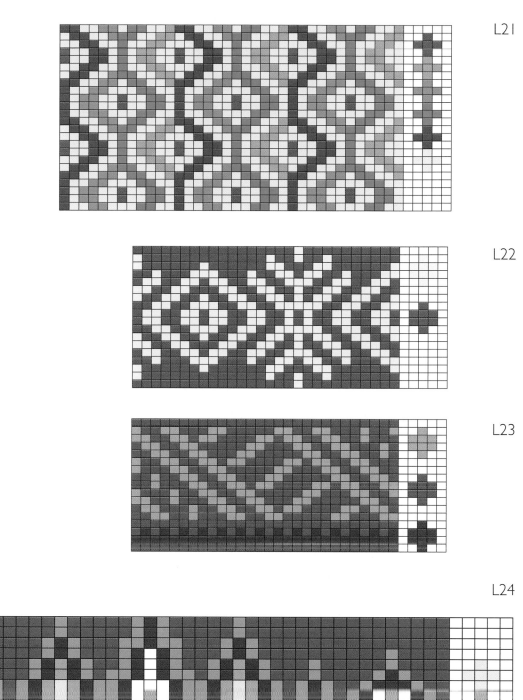

L21

L22

L23

L24

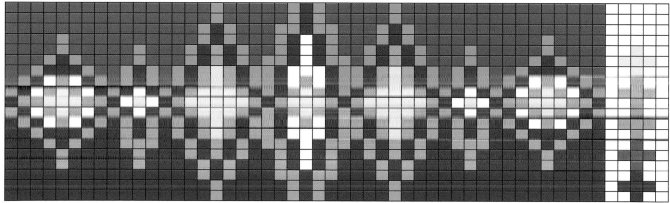

L25

L26

L27

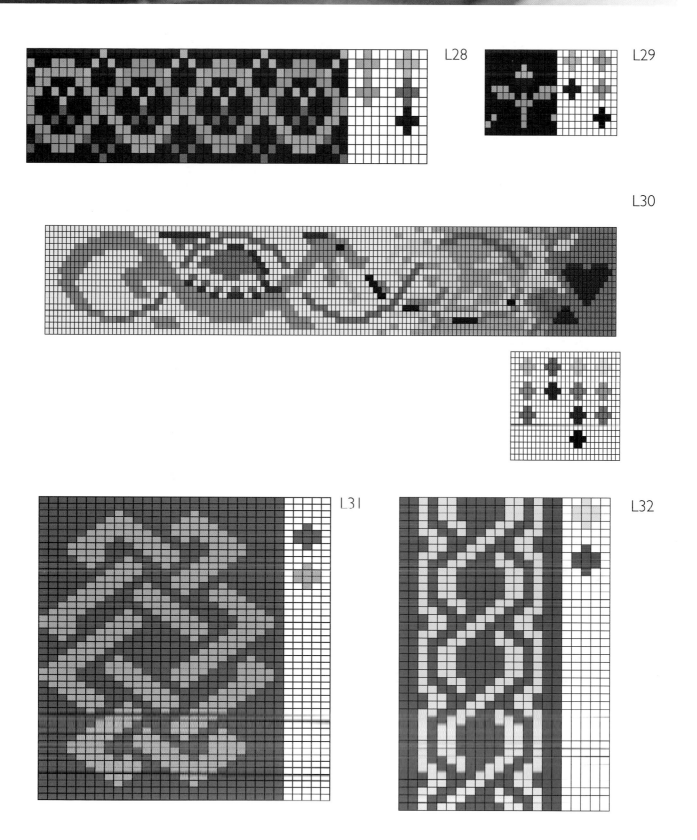

L28

L29

L30

L31

L32

Netting Stitch

N01

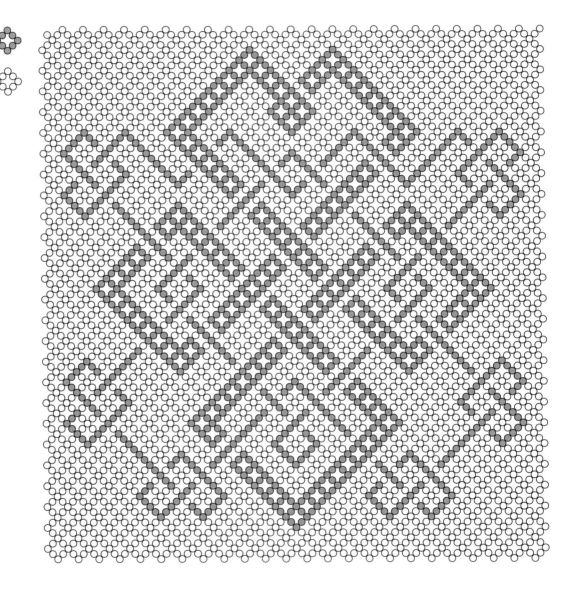

N02

N03

N04

N05

N06

N07

N08

N09

N10

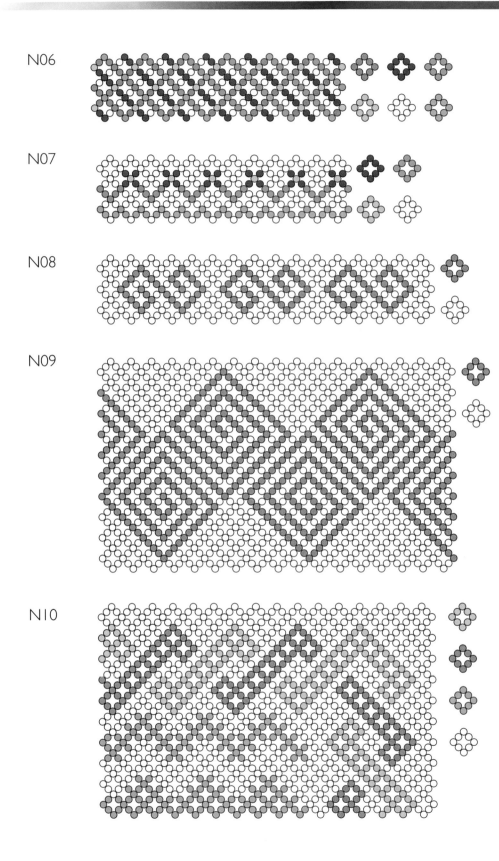

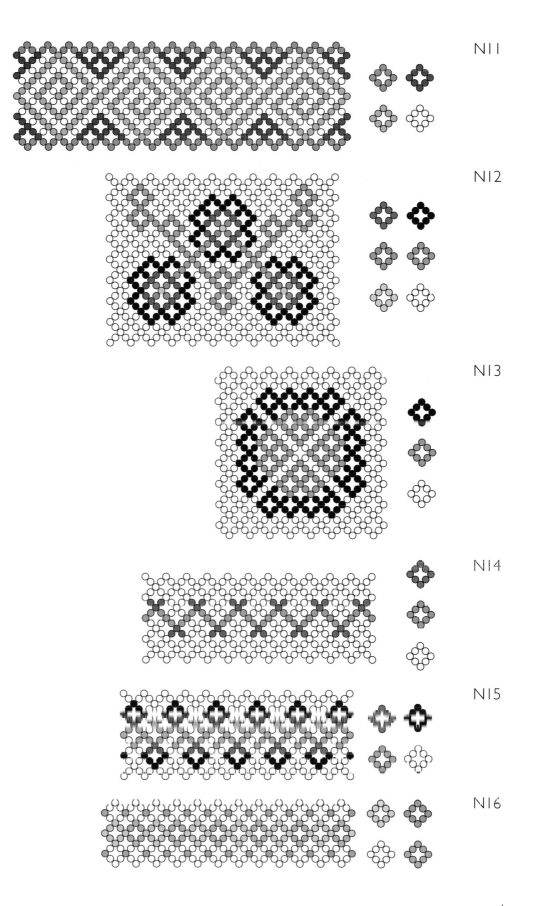

N11

N12

N13

N14

N15

N16

N17

N18

N19

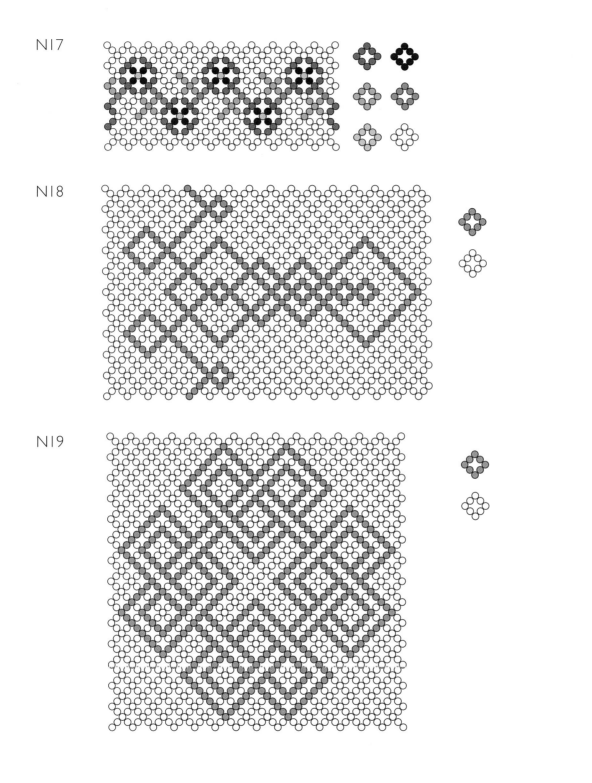

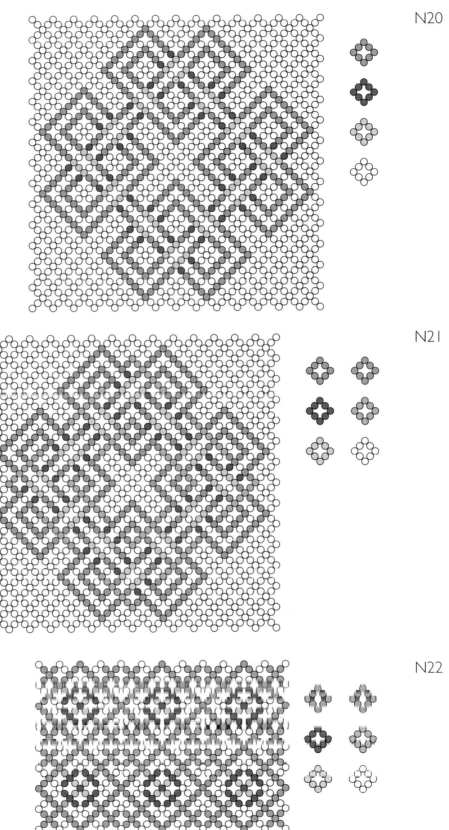

N20

N21

N22

N23

N24

N25

N26

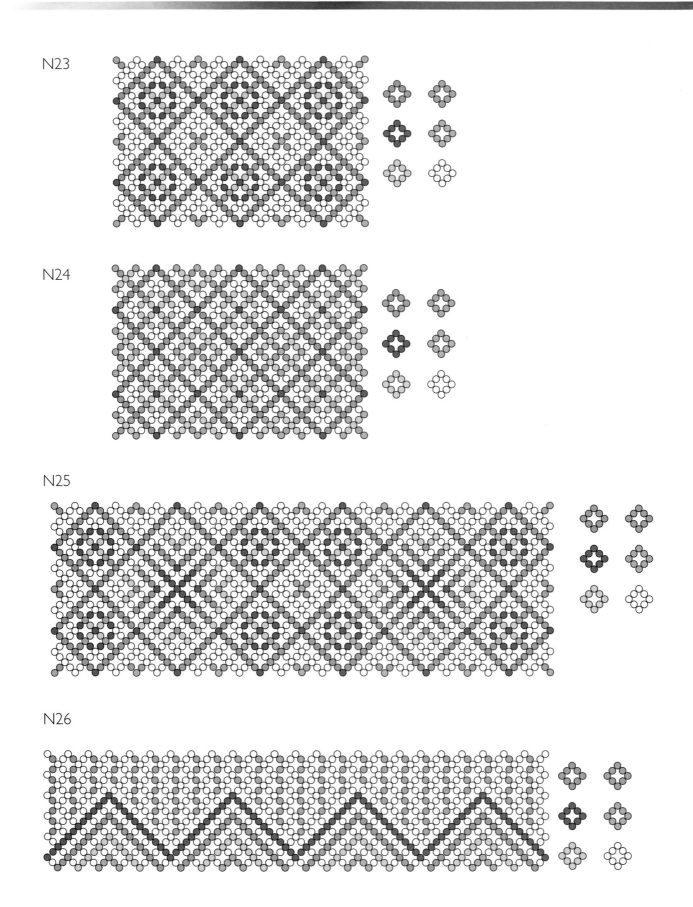

N27

N28

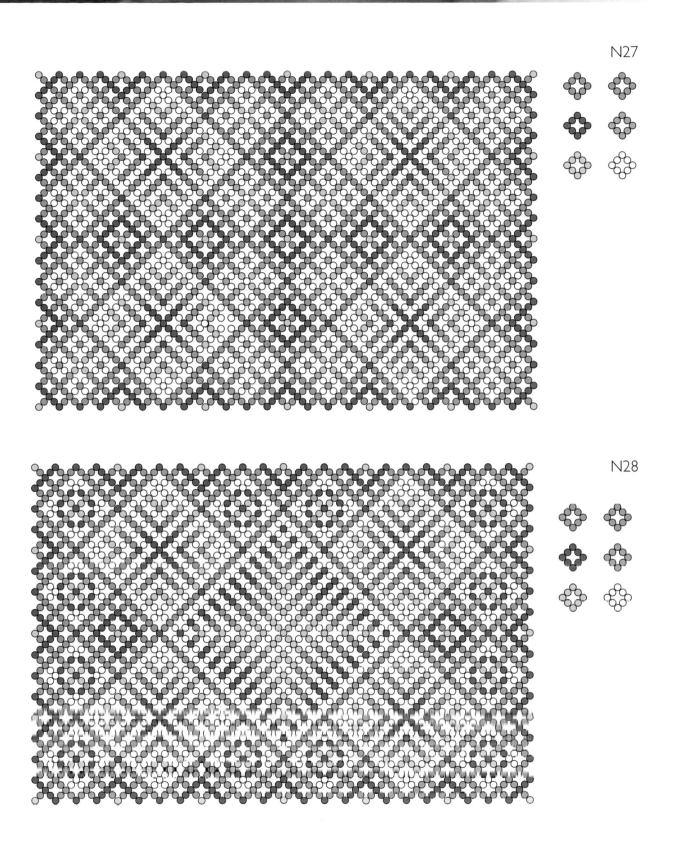

N29

N30

N31

Design Gallery

In this vintage beaded bag, the central design is a repeated mirror-image abstract floral design, with a geometric border across the top of the bag.

Netting is a great stitch to use for a variety of diagonal plaid patterns, such as this amulet bag from *Bead Netted Patterns*.

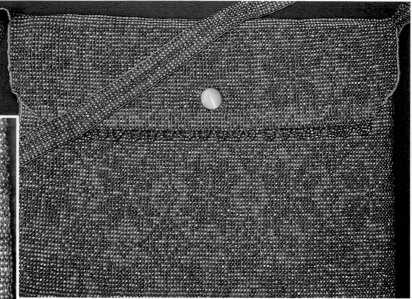

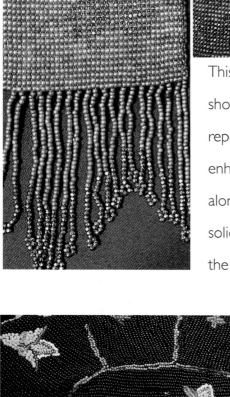

This vintage steel-cut French beaded loomwork purse shows how a small pattern, such as the star design, can be repeated to create an overall design. The purse is enhanced with such details as the simple looped edging along the flap, the striped pattern in the wrist strap, the solid backing with just one star in each bottom corner, and the zigzag fringe.

This vintage clutch purse from Belgium has a couched floral beadwork pattern in size 15 seed beads with steel-cut borders.

This antique steel-cut loomwork beaded bag from the collection of Laura Lauth Williamson has a vibrant symmetrical pattern with a looped twisted fringe, the same as fringe pattern #F04 (page 95).

Here, I have taken a variation of the small leaf pattern #B08 (page 15) and used it as a theme for this forest-themed amulet bag. The colors and fringe reflect the idea of earth and forest.

This beadwork by Margo C. Field entitled "Passion for Paisley" shows a combination of pattern and fringework.

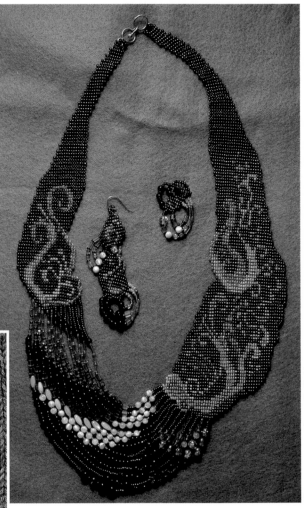

Photo courtesy Margo C. Field

This detail of a vintage beaded bag has a floral center leading into a fan design at the top and small floral design along the bottom.

A very simple geometric pattern with a zigzag fringe embellishment enhances this knitted scarf.

This beautiful antique frame that opens to a box-shape is attached to a basic stripe-patterned bag with loops along the bottom.

An antique bead-crocheted miser's bag shows a simple, small diamond pattern and a geometric border with a metal fringe in a basic rectangle-shape (#111, page 97) with alternating beads at the ends.

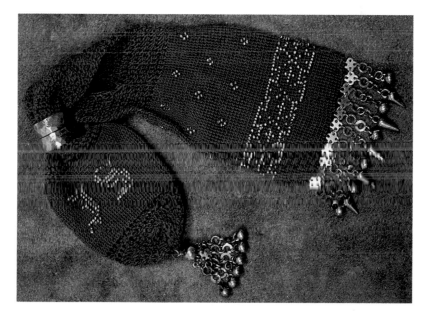

This amulet bag by Corinne Loomer uses a subtle geometric pattern by Brenda Whitehead in *Heirloom Peyote* and then adds an opulent twisted fringe as in fringe pattern #F07 (page 96) and a basic rectangular-shape #F11 (page 97).

This bead-crocheted amulet bag uses a very small leaf pattern in one color of beads and repeats it randomly over the bag surface in different arrangements. The edging along the sides of the bag is the simple looped edging #E02 (page 90).

This antique steel-cut loomwork beaded bag has a geometric and floral pattern with a netted fringe ending in a zigzag pattern at the bottom, as in fringe outline #F16 (page 97).

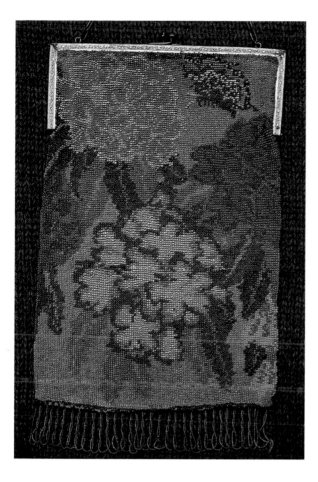

This antique bead knitted purse has been worked up with a different floral and butterfly design on each side.

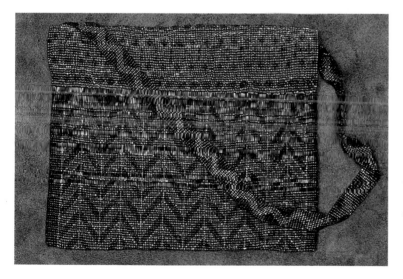

A variety of patterns work well together in this vintage steel-cut art deco purse, from the zigzag along the strap to the chevron shapes for the body of the bag to the curving patterns along the flap.

This original beadwork called "Night Blooms" by Margo C. Field combines basic looped fringe in #F01 (page 94) and simple patterns to create an overall cohesive design.

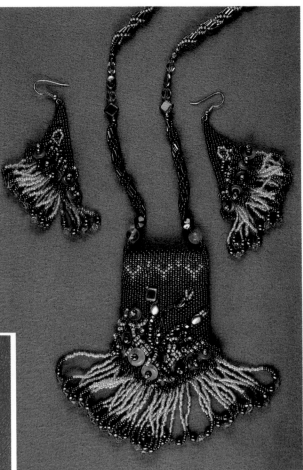

Photo courtesy Margo C. Field

A variety of Celtic patterns in netting create this delicate purse in size 15 seed beads.

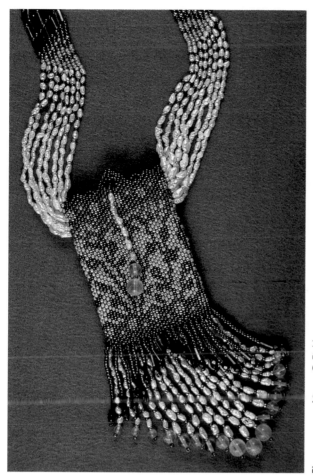

"Seed Bead Weeds" amulet bag by Margo C. Field shows layered fringe and an overall pattern working together as a whole.

Photo courtesy Margo C. Field

This detail of the back of the beaded bag by Delinda Vannebrightyn Amura combines patterns everywhere, from the main design of the tree and pillar motif to the small floral leading into chevrons at the base of the strap.

Cords

Cords can be used for everything from straps on a purse to the focal point of a necklace. They also can be used in every stitch imaginable, many of which are being newly created all the time. Following are patterns for bead-crochet or brick stitch cords and buttonhole stitch cords, as well as an idea list with brief how-to instructions for several other cord techniques.

Crochet Cords

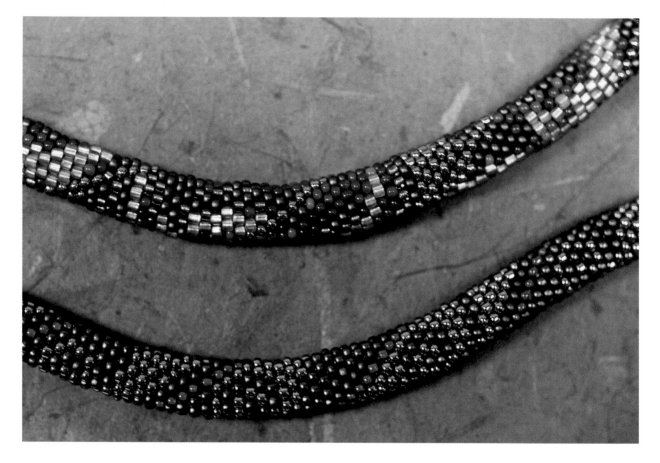

Here are two examples of bead-crochet cords using (top) a portion of #B41 bordered by a gold line of beads and (bottom) #C18 using dark blue and bronze for the blue and cream in the chart.

Crocheted cords have been made for many years, and were especially popular in the 1920s. In recent years, the process has enjoyed renewed interest with all the experimentation with new techniques and patterns of beads. There are many variations of techniques for making crochet cords, from the number of beads in each round to the size and type of thread or cord used to crochet.

The following patterns are for the method of cord crochet that I usually use. The charts use from 10 to 12 beads in each round or row and are strung from right to left, beginning at the top of the chart and working down. You can also string the beads following the chart from left to right, beginning at the bottom of the chart and working up to the top, but this will create a reverse image of the pattern.

I string the approximate number of repeats to complete the pattern and work in the round in slipstitch, sliding the hook through the next stitch the bead is on, pushing the bead to the back of the hook, then sliding one bead down to the work, and completing the slipstitch as usual.

C01

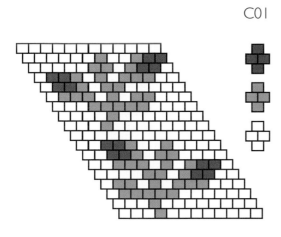

C02

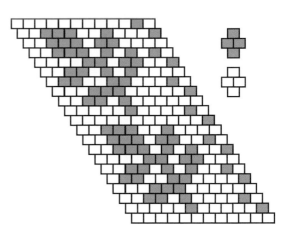

C03

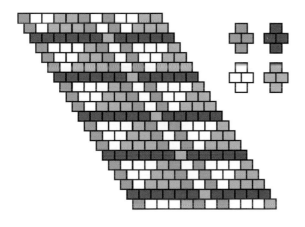

C04

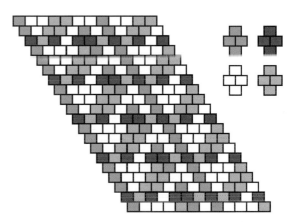

C05

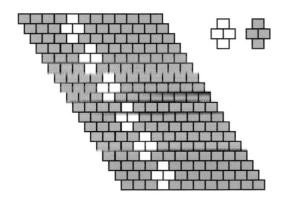

C06

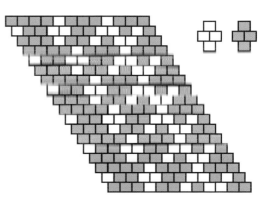

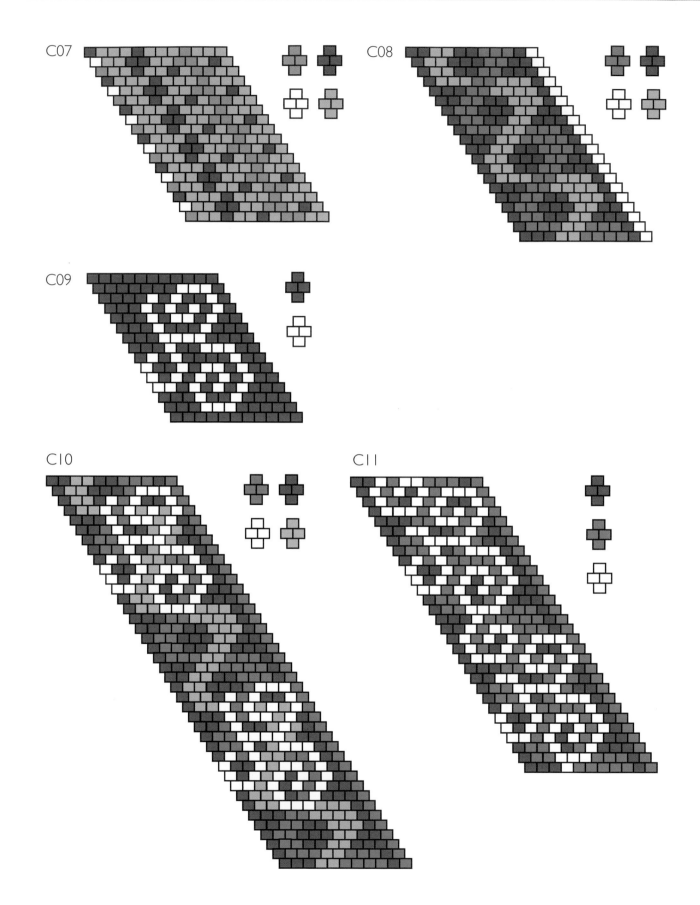

C07

C08

C09

C10

C11

C12

C13

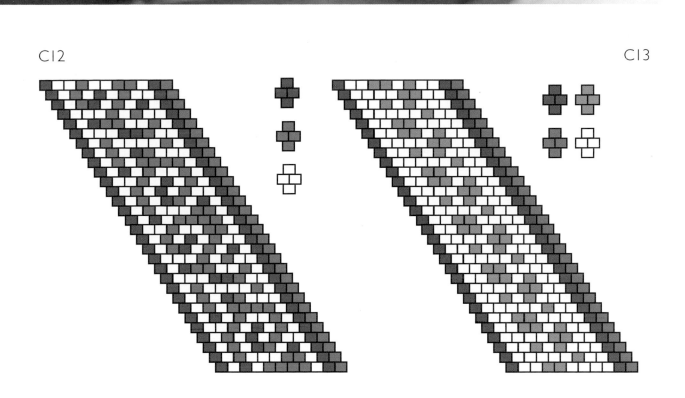

C14

C15

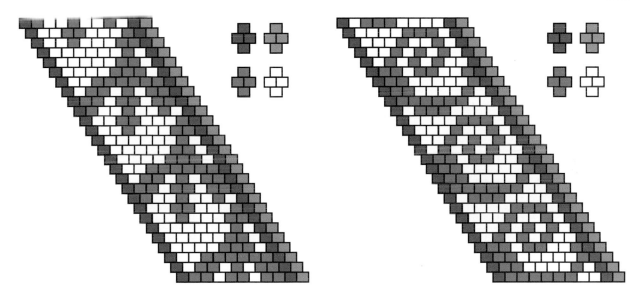

C16

C17

C18

C19

Buttonhole Stitch Cords

Here is a new idea for making cords for bracelets or necklaces. If you know how to embroider in buttonhole stitch, it will help you understand this stitch, since you are simply making buttonhole stitches with a bead slid into each stitch as it is made.

There are two things to remember when working this stitch. The first is to always pass the needle around the thread to the right of the next bead, passing the needle down from top to bottom behind the thread the bead is on, and then over the working thread, as shown in the illustration at right. The second is to pull the thread until the new bead sits below and to the left of the bead you just passed the needle next to, again shown in the illustration. Sometimes, as you pull the thread to tighten it, the thread slips over to the left of the bead that is on the thread, and you need to work it back to the right of the bead. You should not stitch through any beads except when weaving in the ends of the thread.

For step-by-step instructions for this stitch, see the project instructions on pages 116-117 for the Striped Bracelet. To follow the chart for this stitch, add one stitch with a bead for each colored diamond-shape, working each row from left to right, top to bottom.

C20

C21

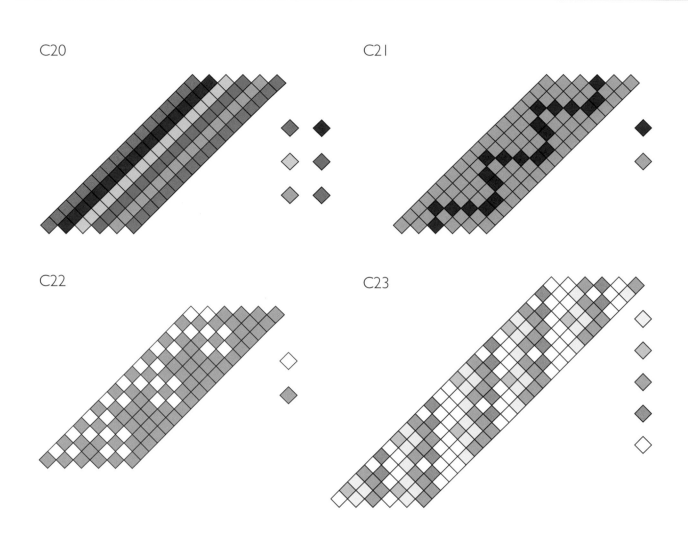

C22

C23

C24

C25

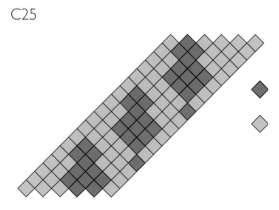

C26

C27

C27

C29

C30

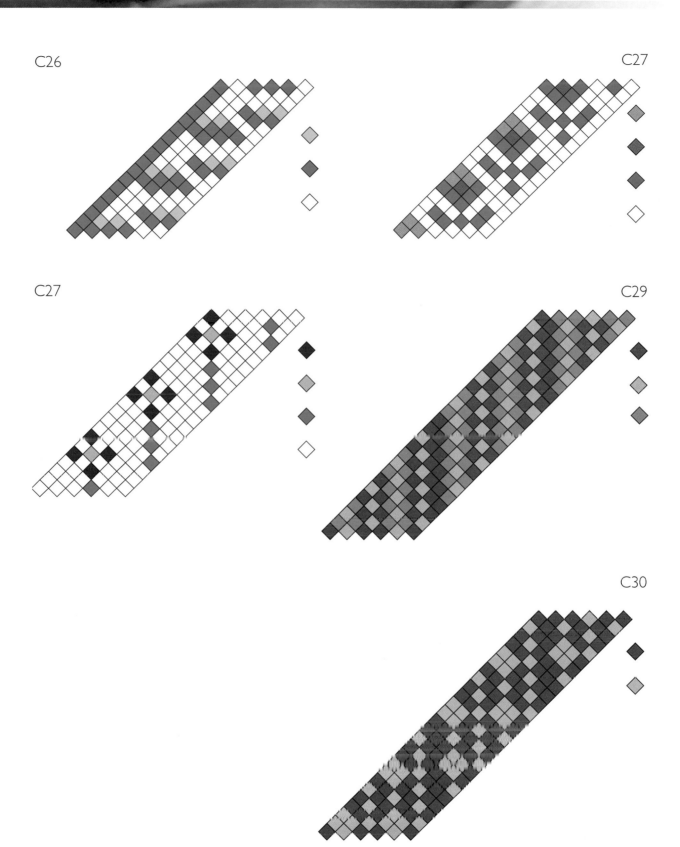

Other Cord Stitches

Following are more ideas for straps and cords. Most of the following techniques are more suited to creative changes in design through variations in bead types and sizes, rather than in charted patterns; therefore, I don't have color charts with these techniques. They still are great options to consider when forming designs, though.

African Helix

This established stitch is not as commonly used, though it is very similar to the buttonhole or half-hitch cord. Because there is more than one bead used in each loop, the variations are most often made in the number, type, and size of beads used in the pattern repeat.

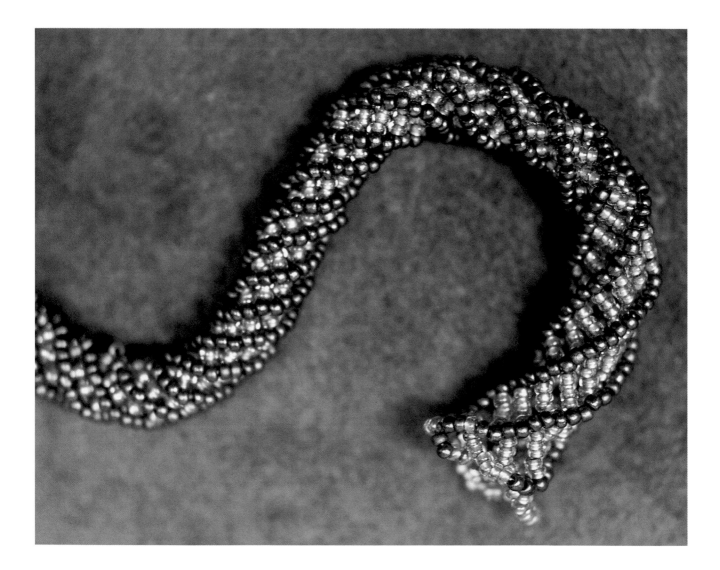

A quick refresher in African Helix:

The easiest way to get used to this stitch is to use two colors of beads and work the first several rows around a pencil. The tighter you pull your stitches, the firmer the tube will be.

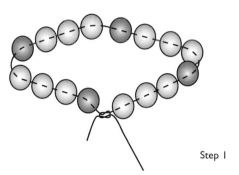

Step 1

1 String four repeats of three light-colored beads and one dark-colored bead. Tie the tail and working thread into a square knot so you have a circle of beads about 6" from the tail end of the thread. Slip the circle of beads onto the pencil.

2 String three light-colored beads and two dark-colored beads. Pass the needle down behind the thread in the circle of beads, after the first three light-colored beads and before the first dark-colored bead, pulling the thread tight so you have a loop of beads with the thread pulled tightly between the beads in the circle.

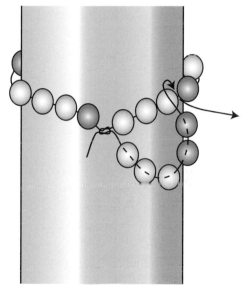

Step 2

3 String three light-colored beads and two dark-colored beads. Pass the needle down behind the thread in the circle of beads, after the next three light-colored beads and before the next dark-colored bead, pulling the thread tight so you now have two loops of beads with the thread pulled tightly between the beads in the circle. Repeat this step once more.

4 To begin the next round, string three light-colored beads and two dark-colored beads. Pass the needle down behind the thread of the loop of beads you added in step 2, passing between the three light-colored beads and the two dark-colored beads. Pull the thread tight until the new loop of beads is in place.

5 Repeat step 4 for each loop of beads around. As you pull the thread through, make sure it stays in place between the groups of light and dark beads. The dark beads will form the spiraling line around the tube as you work. When you've done about three or four rounds, you can slide the tube off the pencil and work the stitches in your hand, manipulating the beads so the thread slides into the correct position as you pull through.

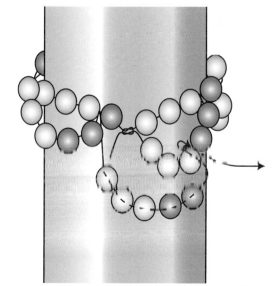

Step 4

Classic Spiral Twist

This is a wonderful old stitch, referred to by several different names, that has many possibilities depending on the size and type of beads you use, as well as the number of stitches you pass through for each repeat.

A quick refresher in Classic Spiral Twist:

The easiest way to work this stitch is to use two colors of beads. When you are comfortable with the stitch, you can vary everything from the number of beads in each loop, to combining sizes and types of beads.

1 String four light-colored beads and three dark-colored beads. Pass back through the all light-colored beads towards the needle end of the thread, creating a loop of beads.

2 String one light-colored bead and three dark-colored beads.

3 Pass through the last three light-colored beads from the first four beads you strung in step 1 and the new light-colored bead from step 2, keeping all the dark-colored beads to the right of the needle as you pass it up through the light-colored beads.

4 String one light-colored bead and three dark-colored beads. Pass through the last three light-colored beads in the growing chain and the light-colored bead you just strung, keeping the dark beads to the right of the needle as you pass it through the beads.

5 Continue step 4, always passing the needle through four beads, three on the growing cord and the one light-colored bead. Always keep the dark beads to the right of the needle as you pass it through the light-colored beads. Your dark beads will spiral around the light bead strand, which will take on a wavy curve.

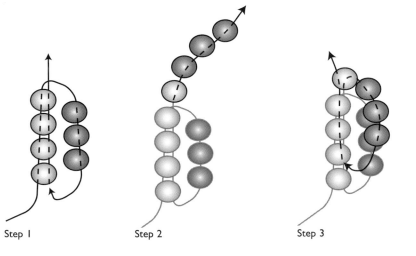

Step 1   Step 2   Step 3

Herringbone Cord (Ndebele Cord)

This is a very speedy cord to make since you are adding two beads for each stitch you work. The herringbone slant the beads take on gives this cord a unique and interesting texture all its own.

Netted Cords

Netted cords have a very fluid stretchy quality that can work very well in necklace and bracelet designs. Varying the size, type, and number of beads in each stitch is one way to vary the design, but you can also add a small pattern, stitch through more or fewer beads for each stitch, and use changing numbers or types of beads in each loop to create new designs.

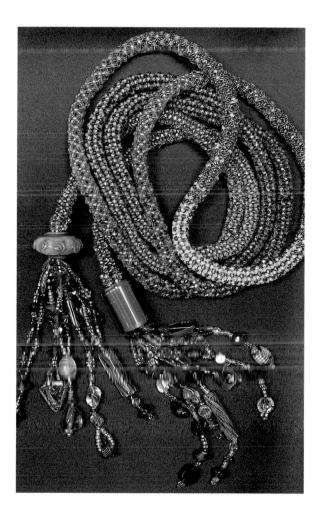

At right, a beautiful use of color in "Ambrosia Lariat" by Liz Smith. Liz has pulled colors from the beads used in the fringe tassels at the end of the lariat and worked them in a graduated pattern of three-bead tubular netting.

In "Dream of the Nymph,"

Delinda Vannebrightyn Amura used

a variety of peyote stitch bands and

cords to create this unique original

work of art.

Peyote Stitch Cords and Bands

A simple band of peyote stitch can make a wonderful neck or wristband. The Fleur-de-lis Gate Purse (page 150) uses a two-bead wide band that is then embellished with beads, pearls, and garnets. The plaid amulet bag on page 59 uses a four-bead-wide band with an easy repeat pattern to complement the bag pattern.

Peyote stitch cords are very versatile in large or small sizes. You can add pattern to this stitch by using portions of any of the brick/peyote charts, or by changing the type and size of the beads in the stitches.

Right-Angle Weave Cord

This stitch is a little more complex to understand at first than some of the other stitches, but once you get the hang of it, it is a very fun stitch to work, creating a cord similar to the peyote stitch cord in feel and drape.

Design Gallery

This project, "Galaxy," by Liz Smith creates a confetti effect by the use of so many different beads.

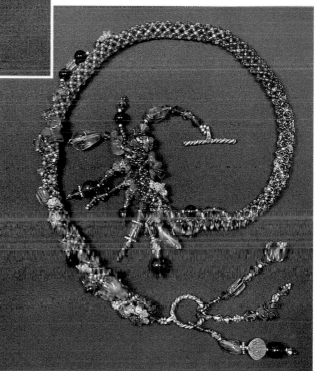

This necklace by Liz Smith closes in front, showing the embellishment on the netted tube cord and the individual dangles that make up the fringe/tassel ends.

Carole Tripp's lariat from the class she took with
Carol Wilcox Wells at the Beads on the Vine 2002
retreat is a great example of the subtleties of color
and how the classic spiral twist cord with an intricate
fringe can make a wonderful design.

These two bracelets are made in buttonhole
stitch. The one on the left uses pattern #C20
(page 76), and the one on the right is
worked in size 5 beads with one drop bead
in each row. When the bracelet was
complete, I stitched over it again with loops
of size 15 seed beads and drop beads.

"Summer Leaf Necklace" by Lisa Taylor
embellishes a right-angle weave tube with
Swarovski crystals and other beads, creating an
elegant chain for the leaf fringe pendant.

This necklace uses a peyote stitch tube, beginning with black size 11 seed beads, graduating to labradorite chips, and then back to the black size 11 seed beads. The fringe is a combination of #F05 and #F09, pages 95 and 96, worked off of a classic spiral rope cord.

In "Botanical Invention" by Margo C. Field, the flowers, which dangle from a simple netted band, are herringbone stitch tubes with branched fringe stems and leaves (#F10, page 96, and #E16, page 92). The stamens are a basic fringe dangle (#F05, page 95).

Detail of "Leaf Motif" by Margo C. Field and "Leaf Motif" matching earrings

Photos courtesy Margo C. Field

This beautiful lariat
by Lisa Taylor
is made in a
herringbone stitch tube.

These two little ladies,

entitled "Head Over Heels,"

by Sylvie Elise Lansdowne employ

a little of everything, from the stripe

and checkerboard patterns, to the

peyote stitch tube legs, to the fringe

and edging ruffles along the skirt, sleeves,

and necks of their outfits.

In "The Journey," Delinda Vannebrightyn Amura has incorporated a variety of patterns and techniques, including surface color patterns, cords, and multi-layered fringes.

At left is an example of a netted tube used for the wrist strap of a purse. I added a little detail of a Celtic knot near the clasp to tie in with the Celtic knot pattern worked on the body of the purse.

Edgings and Fringe

Edgings and fringe are beadwork details that finish off a piece and can add to its personality, ranging from frothy Victorian fringework on a scarf or purse to a simple, tailored clean edge on a book cover or wallet.

I differentiate edging from fringe by its function and form. To me, an edging is short, usually less than ¼" long, and it has the structural purpose of holding two pieces of fabric or beadwork together. Although an edging is often added only as a finishing touch, it is a close and tight enough stitch that it could be structural if needed. Fringe, on the other hand, is longer and its purpose is pure decoration, embellishing the piece and finishing it off. Fringe is almost always stitched more loosely so the individual dangles hang and sway, having a fluid quality, rather than sticking out stiffly at odd angles.

Edgings

From simple brick stitch comes the most common edging in beadwork (#E11), yet there are many other edgings that are less commonly used and just as useful and interesting. Following are several ideas, from stitches over the edge (#E01) to more complex designs.

E03

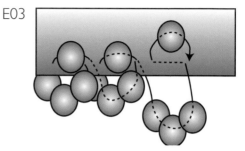

To add a detail to the three-bead edging, you can take a backstitch and add a bead on the top of the fabric or finished beadwork.

E01

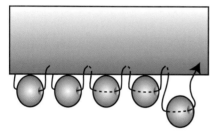

This is the simplest bead edging, where one bead is simply slipped onto the thread before each stitch over the edge of the piece. The bead hole slants from front to back, and the stitch needs to be taken very close to the edge for the beads to stay in place.

E04

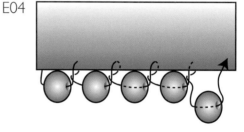

This variation on #E01 lines the beads up along the edge better, since you make a half hitch knot after each stitch.

E02

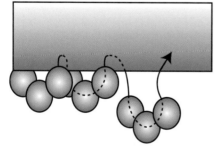

Here, three beads are slid into the stitch. This stitch hides the thread better than #E01, and the beads fit better together along the edge. You can take deeper stitches, using more beads in each stitch and letting the beads cover the whole edge of the fabric or beadwork, creating a thick edge.

E05

Here, three beads are slid into the stitch, just as in #E02. However, since you make a knot after each bead, the beads don't slide over the edge of the work and stay lined up along the bottom edge.

E06

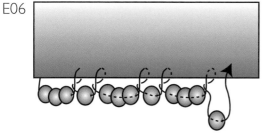

Varying the number of beads in each stitch opens up the possibilities. The single bead could be a drop bead or a crystal, or the three-bead section could be graduated beads.

E09

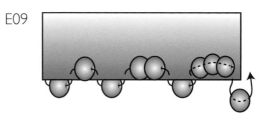

Graduating the number of beads in each stitch can make a nice undulating pattern.

E07

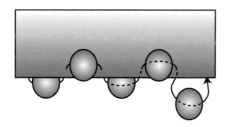

This stitch places one bead on each side of the fabric or beadwork.

E10

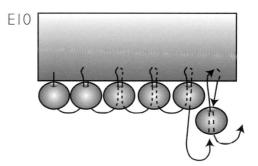

One row of brick stitch worked along the edge can make a nice design as well as be structural.

E08

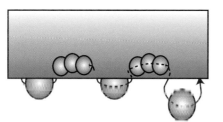

Again, by varying the number of beads, and then the type of beads, you open up all the possibilities of design.

E11

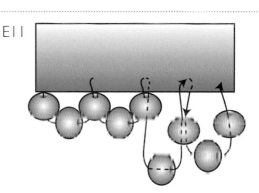

Add an extra bead between your brick stitch and you have the classic edging stitch used by many beaders.

E12

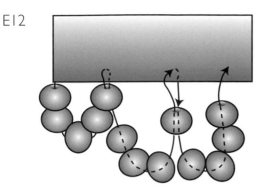

To make the stitch a little longer, add three beads between brick stitches. You can vary this idea by the type of beads you use, making the center bead of the three a different color, size, or type of bead.

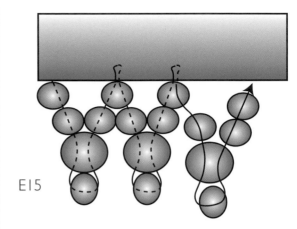

E15

This edging employs the "turnaround bead" used so often in fringe.

E13

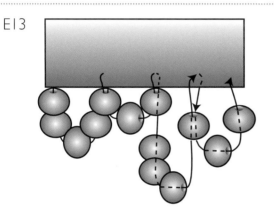

By varying the number of beads between the brick stitches, you increase the options. You could even start with this concept and work into a long fringe.

E16

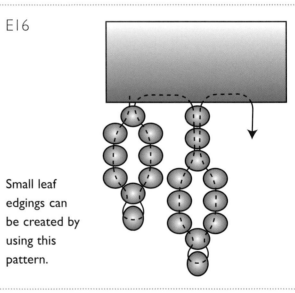

Small leaf edgings can be created by using this pattern.

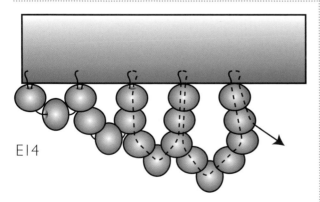

E14

Here is an example of gradually increasing the length by passing through more beads on each successive loop and then tapering back down again.

E17

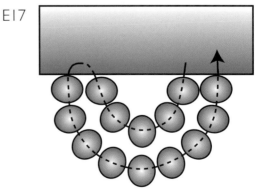

This edging creates a small scallop-shape. Its only disadvantage is that you will need to scoot through some beads or the fabric edging to get into position to make the next scallop.

E18

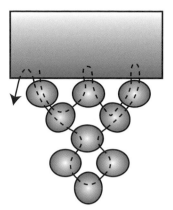

Here is a more intricate picot edging, which combines the basics of #E11 and #E15.

E20

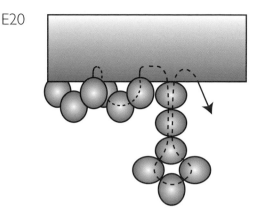

Combining simple and more complex techniques adds interest to edgings, like this combination of #E02 and variation of #E15.

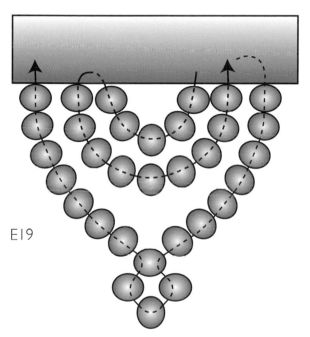

E19

This larger variation of #E17 adds a picot at the center bottom of the pattern.

This purse is edged along the sides in a variation of #E13 (page 91), along the flap in #E15 (page 91), with a straight rectangular twisted fringe as in #F06 (page 96) and #F11 (page 97).

"Beyond the Gate" by Delinda
Vannebrightyn Amura shows a tapered
fringe using alternating dangle patterns
with a smaller layer of fringe on top
tapering in the opposite direction.

Fringe

There are a huge number of designs of fringe. But if you look at them and break them down into the simplest form, there are actually only two basic ways to make the individual dangles that create a fringe.

Individual Dangles

The first—and easiest—way to create fringe is to simply string a strand of beads, followed by a stitch next to the first bead strung, creating a hanging loop of beads. This technique can be varied by the number and type of beads used, as well as by the distance each stitch is made and by all the other techniques that can be worked on fringe.

The other type of fringe occurs when you string a strand of beads, skip the last bead(s) strung (the turnaround bead), and then pass the needle back up through all the other beads so that you create one single hanging strand of beads. This second technique can be varied equally as much as the first, as well as combined with it.

For both of these fringe types, you can twist the strands, work a beadwork stitch on part or all of the strands to thicken them, make branches along the strand, or vary the spacing of the fringe by overlapping or stitching each with large spaces between. Following are a sampling of fringe ideas and some examples of finished fringework.

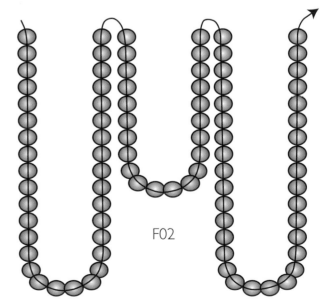

F01

Here is the basic loop fringe, the simplest and easiest of all the fringes to complete.

F02

You can add interest by varying the length of the loops of fringe.

F03

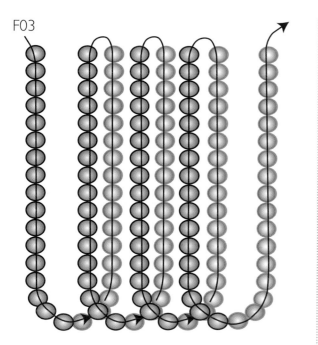

A denser fringe and a different look can be achieved by overlapping the loops as they are stitched in place.

F04

A favorite of antique purse makers, each new strand of beads is passed through the previous loop several times to create a twisted fringe.

F05

This is the most common fringe, made by stringing a length of beads, skipping the last bead (or several beads) strung, and then passing the needle back up through the rest of the beads.
By varying the type and number of beads anywhere along the strand, you can achieve many different designs.

F06

Here, you string a length of beads, skip a bead, pass through a bead, and then string a length of beads equal to the first length and twist the thread until the bead strands kink up, twisting together. Then, you pass through the fabric edge or beadwork to prepare for the next dangle in your fringe. Twisted fringe creates a beautiful edging, though it takes more time than some of the other techniques.

F07

This marriage of #F05 and #F06 (both on page 95) is a nice balance in design, adding a new texture to the straight fringe.

F09

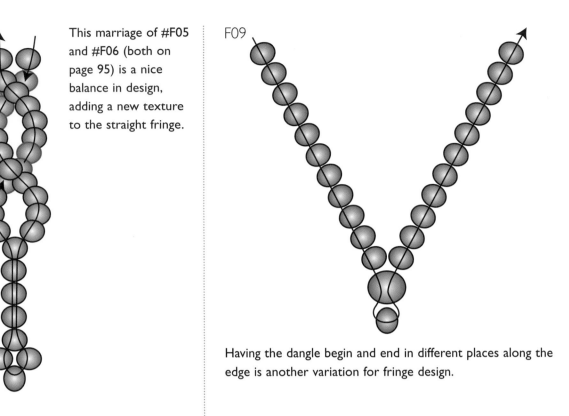

Having the dangle begin and end in different places along the edge is another variation for fringe design.

F08

This dangle design is actually the first step in netting. Using it in a fringe adds width to the dangles, creating a thicker fringe.

F10

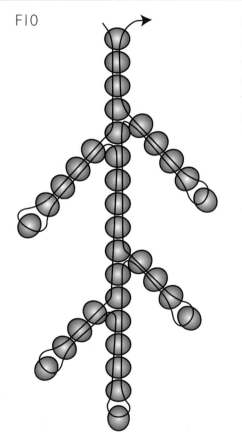

Finally, here is branching fringe, which can be used to make short or long thick texture. It is made by stringing a length of beads, skipping the last bead strung and passing back through some of the beads, then repeating the process to the desired length, and working back up through the main strand, making smaller strands along the way. By using specialty beads, you can make a meandering vine or ocean seaweed.

Fringe Silhouettes

Fringe, because of its large size in proportion to the rest of the piece, needs to be considered as a whole in addition to the consideration you give the individual beads and layout of the dangles you make. The length of the fringe is usually the first consideration in deciding on a design. Then, there is the overall shape of the fringe section, which is most often just rectangle, zigzag, or tapered shapes.

However, there are other possibilities as well. You could use the fringe to frame a special lampwork bead (#F20, page 98), or make it extra long so that it is the main focus of the piece. You also could follow one of the graphed patterns on previous pages to create an image in the fringe pattern.

Following are some basic shape ideas for your fringe and examples of some of the shapes in finished pieces.

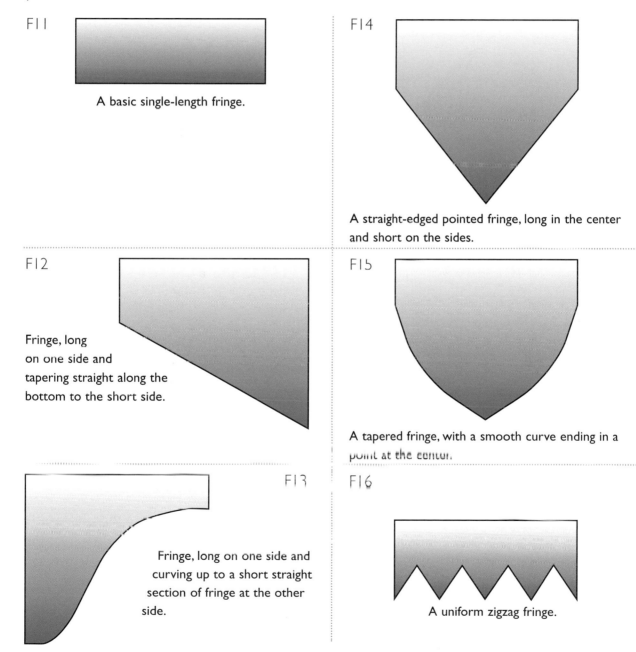

F11

A basic single-length fringe.

F14

A straight-edged pointed fringe, long in the center and short on the sides.

F12

Fringe, long on one side and tapering straight along the bottom to the short side.

F15

A tapered fringe, with a smooth curve ending in a point at the center.

F13

Fringe, long on one side and curving up to a short straight section of fringe at the other side.

F16

A uniform zigzag fringe.

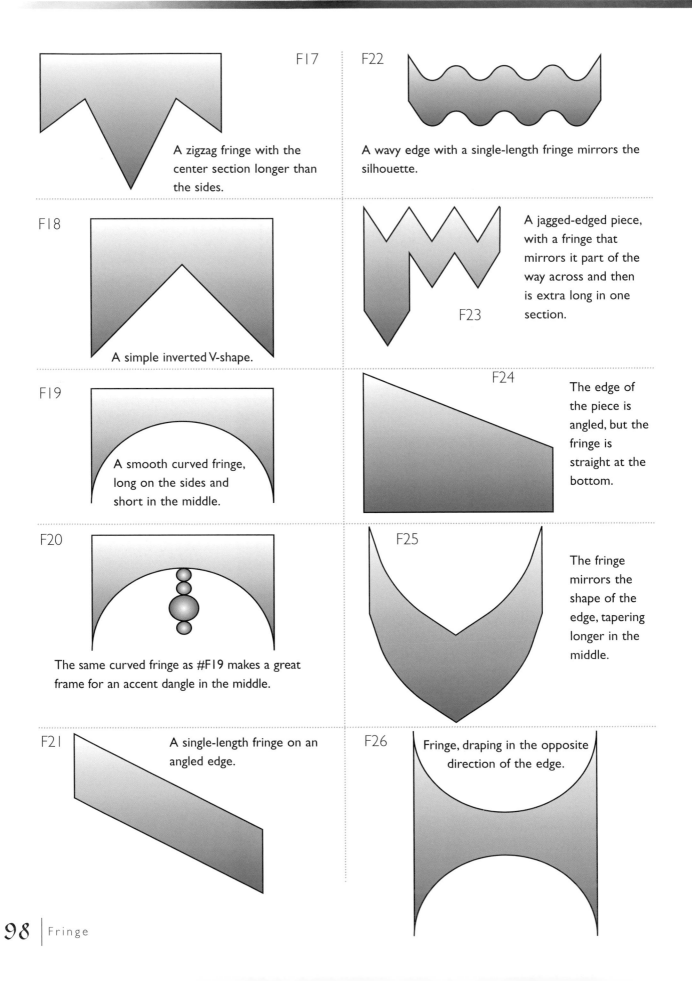

F17 — A zigzag fringe with the center section longer than the sides.

F22 — A wavy edge with a single-length fringe mirrors the silhouette.

F18 — A simple inverted V-shape.

F23 — A jagged-edged piece, with a fringe that mirrors it part of the way across and then is extra long in one section.

F19 — A smooth curved fringe, long on the sides and short in the middle.

F24 — The edge of the piece is angled, but the fringe is straight at the bottom.

F20 — The same curved fringe as #F19 makes a great frame for an accent dangle in the middle.

F25 — The fringe mirrors the shape of the edge, tapering longer in the middle.

F21 — A single-length fringe on an angled edge.

F26 — Fringe, draping in the opposite direction of the edge.

Design Gallery

Liz Smith's "Schehezade," shown here in two color variations, uses a simple peyote stitch ribbon in triangle beads, and then adds a frothy edging, creating a great neckpiece to show off a favorite accent bead.

This finger-knotted lariat by Corinne Loomer boasts tassels at the end made of random arrangements of beads, each dangle creating a unique design.

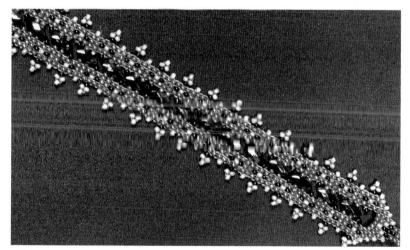

This loomwork bracelet by Kathy Henjyoji uses a very simple pattern accented by a picot edging.

Photo courtesy Margo C. Field

"Deco Red Suede Amulet Bag" by Margo C. Field uses an asymmetrical fringe as in fringe silhouette #F23 (page 98), as well as patterns and edgings.

This ribbon amulet bag by Carole Tripp is edged along the side in one row of brick stitch, edging pattern #E10 (page 91), along the top in #E11 (page 91), with a tapered, partially twisted fringe, #F07 (page 96), shaped as in #F14 (page 97).

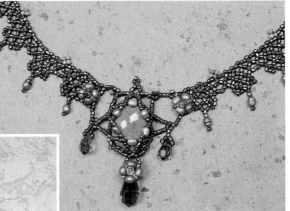

"Romancing the Stone" by
Lisa Taylor uses netting to
create a wonderful romantic
neckpiece. The inner edge is
dotted with little picots,
while the outer edge has
short, simple, basic dangles
(#F05, page 95).

This elegant Victorian-style
loomwork choker by
Kathy Honjyoji adds detail
with the delicate picot edging
leading into the tapering
fringe pattern.

Photo courtesy Margo C. Field

This lariat by Corinne Loomer combines herringbone stitch and a braided strand for the cord, plus polymer clay leaves and various wildlife tassels and accents.

Here is a quick and creative use of fringe by Margo C. Field called "Hair Sticks," dressing up chopsticks for your hair.

Short branching fringes (#F10, page 96) edge this abalone shell bola by Corinne Loomer.

Here are a collection of pieces by Margo C. Field. Clockwise from top left: "Study in Bronze and Blue Amulet Bag," "Santa Fe Angel," "Beaded Bottle Pendant," "Esther Necklace," "White Amulet Bag," "Deco Earrings," "Seascape Amulet Bag," and "August Necklace and Earrings." All are great examples of fringe and pattern combined into a balanced whole.

Projects

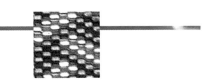

This section features a dozen projects that showcase different ways to use the patterns mentioned earlier in this book. Many of them are simple projects, where just a small amount of beadwork is used to enhance an item. (These can often be some of the most enjoyable projects since they are not as time-consuming or skill-intensive, yet you create something beautiful nonetheless.) Other projects, like the Fleur-de-lis Gate Purse, are more involved.

Dragon Box Band

Here is an example of mirror-image repeats. You could take this design and repeat the pattern in one direction over and over again, or as I did here, when you reach the end (or in this case the middle of the heart), turn around and follow the pattern back in the other direction. In 1999, I entered this box in the Second Miyuki Delica Challenge, sponsored by Caravan Beads of Portland, Maine. The peyote stitch strip is only 18 beads tall, so it works up quickly and can be used to decorate a box as shown, or it can be sewn to a purse, bag, or on a band of clothing. If you or someone you know is interested in Renaissance fairs, the design would look great appliquéd on a vest, belt, or other item to wear to a festival, though purists would agree that the Japanese beads would definitely not be period items!

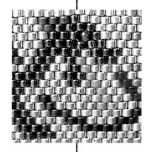

Materials

Finished size of beadwork:

Approximately ⅞" tall x 8¾" long.

- Box or other finished item with a flat area at least 1" high x 9" long
- Size 11 Delica beads in the following colors*:
  - 8 grams gold #041
  - 4 grams bronze #22L
  - 2 grams brown #734
  - 1 gram silver-lined red #602
  - 1 gram olive green #133
  - 2 grams medium green #175
  - 3 grams dark green #327
  - 2 grams purple #323
  - 1 gram yellow/orange #651
  - 1 gram orange #653
  - 1 gram red #723
- Gold-colored beading thread
- Beading needle

*Bead amounts are approximate. You may need slightly more or less depending on your finished piece.

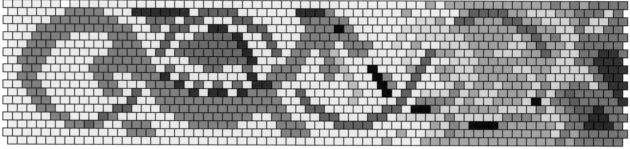

Chart

General Instructions

1 Following the project chart, which is the same as chart #B27 on page 30, begin from the left side of the pattern and work in peyote stitch to the middle of the heart, and then follow pattern back in the other direction to the beginning. Weave in ends.

2 Sew or glue finished beadwork to box or other item.

The inside of the Dragon Box is lined with a netted bead pattern of a twisted rope and a central circular pattern.

Fringe on Organdy Bag

Fringe on Organandy Bag

Here is a quick embellishment to dress up a simple bag, which can be used to hold a special gift, maybe of a handmade beadwork item that uses some of the same beads, for a very, very special friend. I used the basic V-shaped fringe silhouette with a single-dangle design repeated across the bottom of the bag. This is just the beginning, though. You could choose a different fringe silhouette, make layers of fringe, and use up odd beads by making each dangle a little different.

Materials

- Small organdy bag, approximately 3" wide x 4" tall
- 18* size 6 seed beads
- 34* $\frac{1}{8}$"-long twisted hex beads
- 51* size 8 seed beads
- 17* 8mm Swarovski crystals
- 4 grams* size 11 seed beads
- 2 grams* size 15 seed beads
- 17* $\frac{5}{8}$"-long drop leaf beads
- Beading thread (to match beads)
- Beading needle small enough for the size 15 seed beads

*Bead amounts are approximate. You may need slightly more or less depending on your finished piece.

Finished length of fringe section: approximately 2¾" long at center.

General Instructions

1 Thread the needle with a 7-foot length of thread and take a small stitch in the center bottom of the bag. Pull the thread until both ends are the same length, then tie them in a knot to anchor the thread in place.

2 Using the thread end that already has the needle on it, string beads following the bead sequence shown in Figure 1, then pass back through the beads indicated.

3 String another size 6 bead and take a stitch in the fabric one bead's width away from the first size 6 bead. Pass back down through the size 6 bead. Now you are ready to string the next dangle.

4 String the next dangle, following the bead sequence in Figure 1, making the size 11 seed bead section smaller by three beads for each dangle, until you reach the corner of the bag. Tie a small knot and weave in the end.

5 Thread the other end of the thread and repeat the process in the opposite direction.

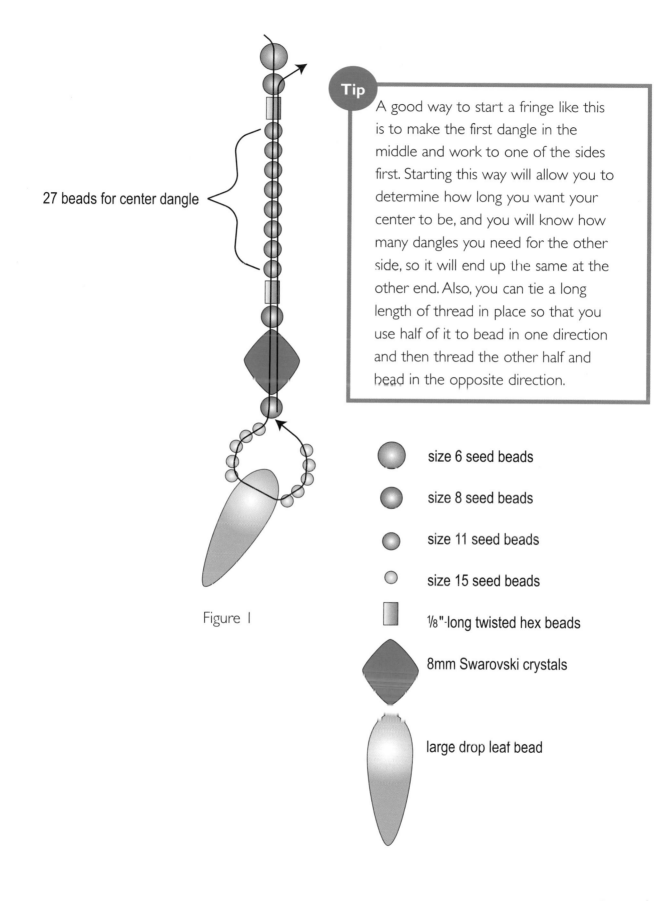

27 beads for center dangle

Tip

A good way to start a fringe like this is to make the first dangle in the middle and work to one of the sides first. Starting this way will allow you to determine how long you want your center to be, and you will know how many dangles you need for the other side, so it will end up the same at the other end. Also, you can tie a long length of thread in place so that you use half of it to bead in one direction and then thread the other half and bead in the opposite direction.

size 6 seed beads

size 8 seed beads

size 11 seed beads

size 15 seed beads

⅛"-long twisted hex beads

8mm Swarovski crystals

large drop leaf bead

Figure 1

Striped Bracelet

This easy-to-make bracelet is simply buttonhole stitch worked around a pencil, with a bead slipped into every stitch as you go. Using six size 8 or larger beads around, and making a tube using a pencil as a base, the stitches are loose enough so that when you take the tube off the pencil, you have a fluid drape in the bracelet with enough give for the bracelet to stretch a little to slide over your hand. It's easiest when you use the standard hexagon-shaped pencil,  because then you have one bead on each hexagon section, so in the beginning, when it's always a little confusing in beadwork, it's easier to see where you are in the round. Using varying sizes of beads makes the undulating pattern on this example. Another example of this type of bracelet is included at the end.

Finished size:
approximately ⅝" wide.

Materials

- 4 grams* each of a variety of beads similar to the following:
  - Size 11 blue seed beads
  - Size 8 blue seed beads
  - Size 6 blue-and-white-striped seed beads
  - Size 5 dark blue triangular beads
  - Size 6 black-lined clear AB beads
  - Size 8 blue-green hex beads
- Pencil
- Beading thread (in a color close to or darker than most of the beads used)
- Beading needle

*Bead amounts are approximate. You may need slightly more or less depending on your finished piece.

General Instructions

1 Tie a 9-foot length of thread around a pencil, making a square knot and leaving a 6" tail to weave in later. Position the tail above your work so it won't get caught up in the progressing beadwork.

2 Working in a counterclockwise direction, pick up a bead and pass the needle through the loop of thread, to the right of the bead, as shown in Figure 1. This is the first purple diamond-shape in the row (upper left corner) of the pattern chart.

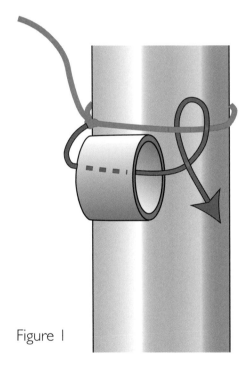

Figure 1

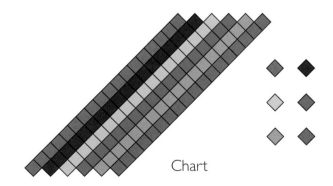

Chart

3 Repeat step 2 around the thread on the pencil, adding one bead of each type (six beads total). The first row of the chart is now complete.

4 Begin the spiral pattern by adding the next bead
to the right of the first bead you strung, and
using the same type of bead as the bead that is
on the stitch you will be passing the needle
through, as shown in Figure 2. Pull the thread
tight so the new bead lines up just below and to
the left of the first bead . Repeat until the tube,
when stretched slightly, equals the measurement
around the widest part of your hand
(this is usually about 7½" to 8½"). Make sure
the last bead you add is the last bead in the
bead sequence that you started out with.

5 Slide the tube off the pencil and line up the
ends so the pattern continues in a spiral. Weave
through the beads at the joint several times,
making knots and sliding through beads until
the bracelet is seamed together. Weave in ends.

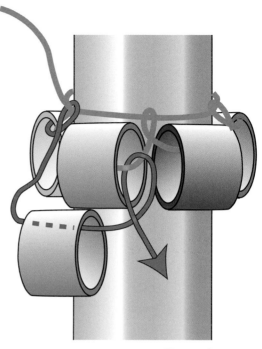

Figure 2

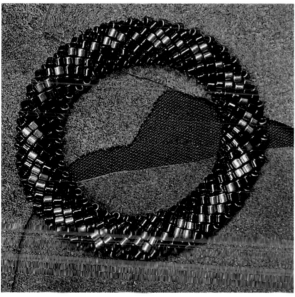

Using the same technique as
the Striped Bracelet, this
bracelet is worked in pattern
#C30 below.

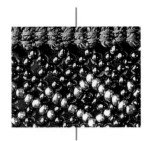

Sometimes, a small, simple pattern is all you need to make something special. This netted band of cabling adds a lot to this gourd bowl.

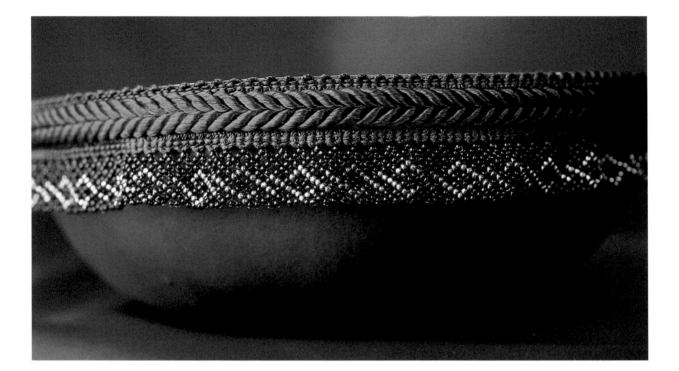

Green-and-Gold Netting Border on Gourd Bowl

Materials

- Gourd bowl, about 8" diameter, painted and varnished
- Decorative trim long enough to go around the bowl
- 6 grams* green size 11 seed beads
- 3 grams* bronze size 11 seed beads
- Green beading thread
- Beading needle
- Sewing needle and green thread
- Tacky Glue

  *Bead amounts are approximate. You may need slightly more or less depending on your finished piece.

Finished size: ½" tall.

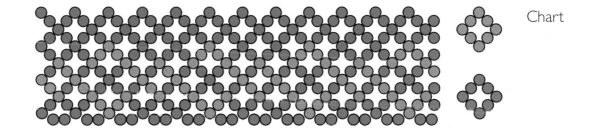

Chart

General Instructions

1 Fit the trim around the top edge of the bowl, overlapping the ends about ½", and cut excess trim beyond the ½" overlap.

2 Remove trim from the bowl and sew the overlapping section together with the sewing needle and thread.

3 Thread the beading needle with a 6-foot length of beading thread and take a small stitch in the bottom edge of the trim. Tie the tail, working thread into a knot with a 6" tail to weave in later.

4 Following the cable-netting chart, repeat the netting pattern around the trim. Weave in ends.

5 Glue the trim to the top edge of the bowl.

Scissors Chatelaine

This elegant beaded chatelaine is an example of an edging used both for decoration and for function. The Ultrasuede pieces are held together by the decorative beaded edging. The example uses black beads to contrast the red Ultrasuede, but you could use coordinating beads instead. Also, using larger beads or making the stitches closer together along the edge of the suede will create a ruffled effect.

Finished size: 1½" wide x 3¾" long, not including neck chain.

Figure 1

Figure 2

Figure 3

Materials

- 2 1¼" x 3¼" pieces of Ultrasuede or suede
- 45* ⅛"-long faceted beads
- 8 ½"-long black beads
- 6 size 6 black seed beads
- 5 size 8 red seed beads
- 12 ½"-long x ⅛"-wide red bugle beads
- 4 grams* size 8 black triangle beads
- 4 grams* ⅛"-long red twisted hex beads
- 4 grams* size 11 metallic red seed beads
- 4 grams* size 11 black seed beads
- Scissors
- Tracing paper and pen
- Several paperclips

*Bead amounts are approximate. You may need slightly more or less depending on your finished piece.

General Instructions

1 Using the pattern in Figure 1, trace the front and back onto the tracing paper and cut out the shapes to create patterns.

2 Place the patterns on the suede, mark around them with pen, and cut out.

3 Fold front piece over along the dotted line on the pattern. Stitch six black size 11 seed beads across fold to hold the fold in place, as shown in Figure 2.

4 Line up the front and back suede using paperclips to hold in place.

5 Begin picot edge as shown in Figure 3, making stitches about ³⁄₁₆" apart on the suede, or make them closer together to make a ruffled edge. (Note: You will need more of the small faceted beads to make the ruffled edge option.) At the center bottom, use two size 8 red beads and one size 6 black bead for the center bottom picot, instead of the faceted bead (see photo of finished project).

6 Continue up the other side and around the back of the piece of suede to the beginning. End by stitching into the first bead in the pattern along the edge.

7 Stitch the center detail through the six beads along the front, as shown in Figure 4.

8 Attach a 5-foot length of thread to the side of the chatelaine at the fold in the front and string the neck chain, following the pattern in the photo of the finished project or creating your own pattern. Take a stitch in the opposite side of the chatelaine and pass back through all the beads in the neck chain, adding more beads if desired, then weave in the thread.

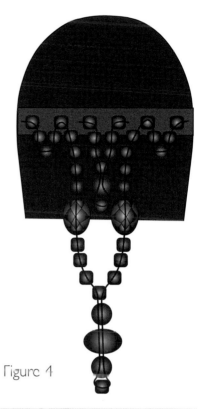

Figure 4

Peyote Stitch Key Chain

These little key chains are fun and quick to make, and are very versatile too. They are a good project when you want to try out color combinations and make something useful at the same time, to teach someone how to do a little beadwork, or to make a small gift of beadwork. You can write a tiny message on the bottom of the wood base, then hide it with a long fringe, or make a short looped edging. You can use them as Christmas ornaments, tassels, or zipper pulls. Make the simple edging in the instructions, or follow any of the fringe patterns to make a more ornate edging or fringe as shown in the photo of key chains. The instructions were originally written for a beginner's project, so they are great for a new beader.

Finished size:

½" wide x 1" tall,
not including fringe or
jump rings.

Materials

- 4 grams* each of size 11 Delica beads as follows:
  - dark blue purple #696
  - medium blue #693
  - teal #608
  - gold #34
- 14 size 8 seed beads
- 1"-tall wooden "milk can" base
- Size 11 beading needle
- White beading thread
- ½"-long screw eye
- 1 small (about ½") jump ring
- 1 large (about ⅞") jump ring
- Hammer and nail
- Pliers
- Scissors
- Clear fingernail polish or paint and varnish (optional)

*Bead amounts are approximate. You may need slightly more or
less depending on your finished piece.

General Instructions

Before the beading:

1 The wooden key chain can be used unfinished, or painted and
varnished. Clear or colored fingernail polish works great.
Only the top rim needs to be painted. You can also write a
little message on the bottom of the wood base, which is
especially nice if it's a gift.

2 Next, using a nail and hammer, tap an indentation in the top
center of the wood base.

3 Screw a screw eye into the wood base at the indentation you
made with the nail. Holding the screw eye with a pair of pliers
and twisting the wood base, while resting it on a table, makes
this process easier. Do not screw the screw eye in beyond the
threads on the screw eye or you may break the screw eye.

4 Attach the small jump ring to the screw eye and the large
jump ring to the small jump ring. Now you are ready to begin
beading.

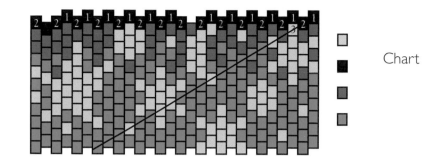

Chart

Completing the project:

1 Onto a 6-foot piece of thread, string 26 dark blue beads. String through the beads again to form a circle, being careful not to pierce the thread already through the beads, as shown in Figure 1.

2 Leaving a 6" tail, tighten the ring of beads around the base, as shown in Figure 2. Tie a square knot.

3 Beginning at round three on the pattern, pick up a gold bead, skip the first bead on the ring, and pass the needle through the next bead on the ring, as in Figure 3. Pull tight.

4 Repeat step 3 four more times, following the color pattern on the graph from right to left (reverse if left-handed).

5 When adding the sixth bead, don't skip a bead on the wood base, just pass through the next bead, as shown in Figure 4. This bead will sit at an angle until the next round, and is shown on the graph without a bead above it because it will make a new vertical line of beads.

6 Continue in basic peyote stitch, adding six more beads, and then make one more increase stitch, as in step 5.

7 For the last bead in the round, pass the needle through two beads to get the needle in position for the next round, as shown in Figure 5. This maneuver shifts where you begin the round by one bead. The graph is marked with a diagonal line to indicate this changing first bead position.

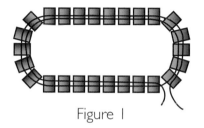

Figure 1

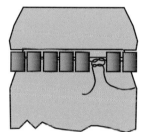

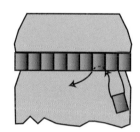

Figure 2

Figure 3

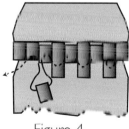

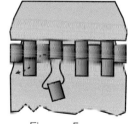

Figure 4

Figure 5

(continued)

8 Continue basic peyote stitch (no more increases), following the design graph for the remainder of rounds.

9 After the final round from the graph, begin the bottom edging by adding four small beads, one large bead, four small beads, and then pass the needle through the third bead away on the previous round of the base. Continue around in the same manner, three times around, until there is a loop entering and exiting every bead on the bottom round of peyote stitch. You will need to pass over the loops before adding the nine-bead loop and pass under the loops before passing the needle through the bead on the wooden base to make the loops overlap each other, as shown in Figure 6.

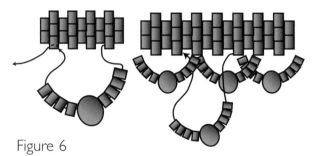

Figure 6

10 To hide the excess threads, pass the needle through the beads on the base of the key chain, then change direction and weave through several more, as shown in Figure 7. Repeat so that about 2" of thread is woven into the beads and the thread has passed over itself once or twice. Cut the thread as close as possible to the beadwork.

Figure 7

Crochet Bracelet and Necklace

This bead-crochet necklace and bracelet set are made using the small rosebud pattern #C01, page 71. They are examples of how you can take any of the brick/peyote stitch patterns and use them for bead-crochet tubes. The size 15 beads for the bracelet and size 11 beads for the necklace are worked 12 beads around, rather than the usual six beads. That way, there is more room for the pattern.

Finished size: (bracelet) 8½" long, depending on beads and clasp;

Materials

Bracelet

- Size 15 seed beads* as follows:
  - 4 grams medium green
  - 3 grams lavender
  - 10 grams of cream
- 110 yards of 1,000 denier silk cord
- Size 10 crochet hook
- 2 silver cone beads
- 2 ½" accent beads
- Toggle and loop clasp
- Beading needle
- Beading thread (in color to match background beads)

*Bead amounts are approximate. You may need slightly more or less depending on your finished piece.

Note

If you prefer not to use the silk cord for the bead and clasp section, or your beads have holes that are too small for the thread to fit through, weave in the end of the thread when you have finished crocheting, and attach your favorite beading thread to string the beads and clasp in step 3.

General Instructions

1 To make the bead-crochet section, string the beads onto the silk, following the pattern in the chart, stringing each row of beads from right to left (begin at the arrow), working from the top row of the chart to the bottom of the chart. Repeat the pattern seven times.

2 Begin your crochet with an 18" tail, so you can use that thread to string the other beads and clasp on later. Work bead-crochet, slipstitching in front of the previous bead and sliding a new bead into each stitch, 12 stitches around, until all the beads have been crocheted.

3 Pull the thread through the last loop and cut thread to 18".

4 Thread the needle with one of the 18" lengths of thread and string the cone and beads onto the thread and one part of the clasp. Pass back through the beads and anchor the thread in the crochetwork.

5 Pass back through the beads and the clasp and then back to the crochetwork. Weave in the end.

6 Repeat steps 4 and 5 for the other end of the bracelet.

Materials

Necklace

- Size 11 seed beads* as follows:
  - 4 grams medium green
  - 3 grams lavender
  - 10 grams cream
- 4 cone or doughnut beads (for ends of crochet sections)
- 2 ½" or larger accent beads
- 4 ½" disk beads
- 8 ½" faceted green pearls
- 10 silver cap beads (for pearls)
- Variety of size 6 or equivalent beads in purples and greens
- Size 8 cream pearl cotton
- Size 10 crochet hook
- Green beading thread
- Beading needle
- Clasp

*Bead amounts are approximate. You may need slightly more or less depending on your finished piece.•

Finished size: (necklace, crochet section) 7½" long.

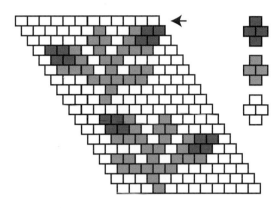

Chart for necklace and bracelet

General Instructions

1 Work the crochetwork the same as for the bracelet, except string six-and-a-half repeats of the design, instead of seven repeats, and weave in the ends of the pearl cotton when done.

2 Attach the beading thread at one end of the crochetwork. Following the pattern sequence in the project photo of the finished necklace or using your own design, string your beads and one end of the clasp, measuring from the center of the crochetwork to the clasp to determine half the finished desired length.

3 Pass back and forth through the beads at least once more for strength, and then weave the end into the crochetwork.

4 Repeat steps 2 and 3 for the beads and clasp on the other side of the necklace.

Brick Stitch Art Deco Purse

This project shows how you can take a pattern and edit it to fit what you want to make. It is also an example of a limited amount of beadwork used to embellish a larger project. The three hanging beads on this purse inspired the color choices for this project and the art deco style design is a favorite in my family. This relatively large

purse takes much less time to make than a fully beaded purse and is a nice size in the size 8 seed beads. If you made the same beadwork design in size 11 seed beads, it would fit on the similar small pinch purse frames available.

Materials

- Size 8 seed beads* as follows:
  - 40 grams light blue charlottes
  - 7 grams copper-colored
  - 14 grams medium blue
  - 6 grams silver-colored
  - 5 grams gold-colored
- 3 ½" accent beads
- 5½" to 6" hinged purse frame
- 16"-wide x 21"-long fabric piece
- Post-It Notes®

*Bead amounts are approximate. You may need slightly more or less depending on your finished piece.

Finished size of beadwork:
5¾" wide x 6" long.

General Instructions

1 Using Post-It Notes, frame off the desired bottom shape of the art deco pattern on page 21 or use the edited chart shown here.

2 Stitch the beadwork, decreasing where you have framed off the design or following the decreases shown on the chart. Weave in ends.

3 To make the fabric purse, first finish the ends before making the casing. To do this, fold the ends of the 21" sides over ⅛", then ¼" for 2½", tapering to the raw edge after the 2½" section. Stitch with a ³⁄₁₆" seam.

4 Fold the 16"-wide ends over ¼", then 1", and sew a casing ⅞" from the last fold.

5 Fold the fabric in half, right sides together so that the casings meet, and sew a ½" seam along the sides up to the ³⁄₁₆" finished edge section.

6 Follow the directions for your purse frame to assemble the frame and slide the fabric in place.

7 Stitch the finished beadwork to the gathered fabric of the purse, just below the frame section.

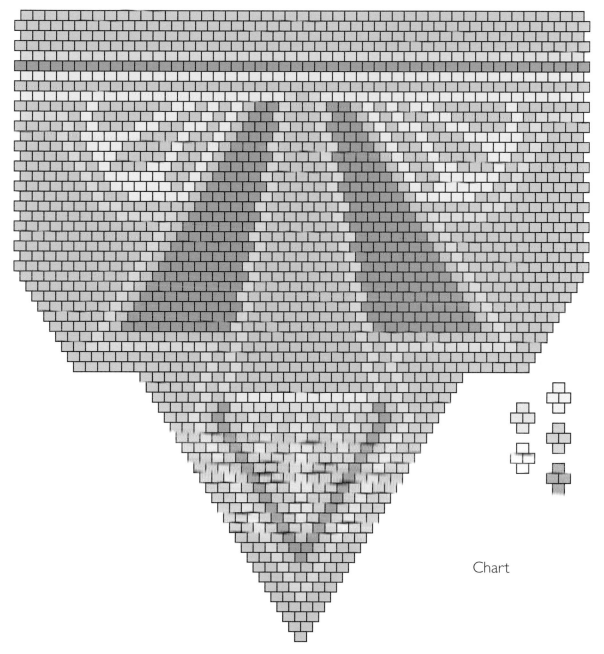

Chart

Thread Spool Scissors Holder Pin Cushion

Here is an example of using a small part of a larger pattern to give the feel of the pattern, yet create an abstract look as well. The leaf pattern #B41 (page 31) was cropped and worked in the round on the spool, and then a coordinating fabric was used for the pincushion. The beading portion of this project is the same process as the key chain project (page 125), and the fabric pincushion is just a huge old-fashioned yo-yo stuffed with batting or stuffing.

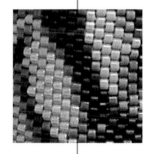

Finished size:

2⅛" tall x 4½" wide.

Chart

Materials

- 1½" wide x 2⅛" tall wooden spool, painted and varnished
- 4 grams* each size 11 Delica beads in the following colors:
  - yellow #160
  - yellow/green #733
  - light green #877
  - medium green #724
  - deep green #656
  - dark green #797
  - darkest green #327
  - gold #041
- 9" circle of fabric
- Polyester stuffing
- Elastic sewing thread and chenille needle (with eye large enough to accommodate elastic thread)
- Beading needle
- White beading thread

*Bead amounts are approximate. You may need slightly more or less depending on your finished piece.

General Instructions

1 Onto 6-foot thread length, string 80 gold beads. String through the beads again to form a circle, being careful not to pierce the thread already through the beads, as shown in Figure 1.

Figure 1

2 Leaving a 6" tail, tighten the ring of beads around the base, as shown in Figure 2. Tie a square knot.

3 Work in peyote stitch around for each row until you have finished working the pattern. Weave in the tail thread.

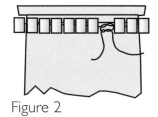

Figure 2

4 To make the pincushion, fold the edge of the fabric circle under about ½", and using the elastic thread and chenille needle, make ¼"-long stitches along the edge of the fold all around the circle. Overlap the first and last stitch, and then pull the thread to gather the fabric into a bag-shape.

5 Using the beading thread and needle, sew the gathered edge of the fabric to the bottom row of the beadwork.

6 Cut a 1" round hole in the center of the fabric circle and stuff the fabric with the polyester fill, making a doughnut-shape and leaving the center bottom area free of stuffing. As you are stuffing, make sure stuffing is evenly distributed.

7 Slide the 1" hole in the fabric over the bottom of the spool as if the spool was a button and you were pushing it through a buttonhole. It should be a tight fit as this is what holds the pincushion in place at the bottom. You may need to cut a small slit in the hole to get it to stretch over the spool, but be careful not to cut it too big.

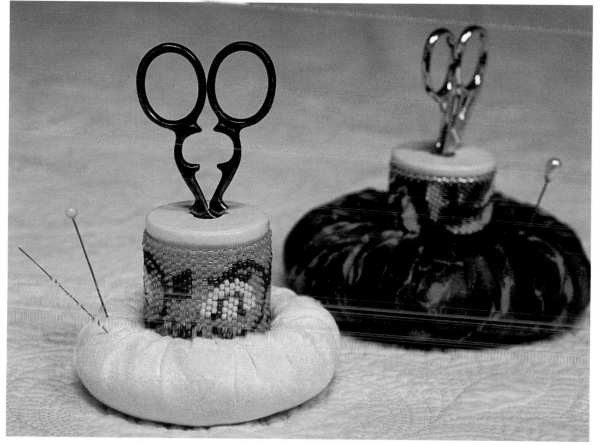

To make a smaller pin cushion, use a 7" circle of fabric.

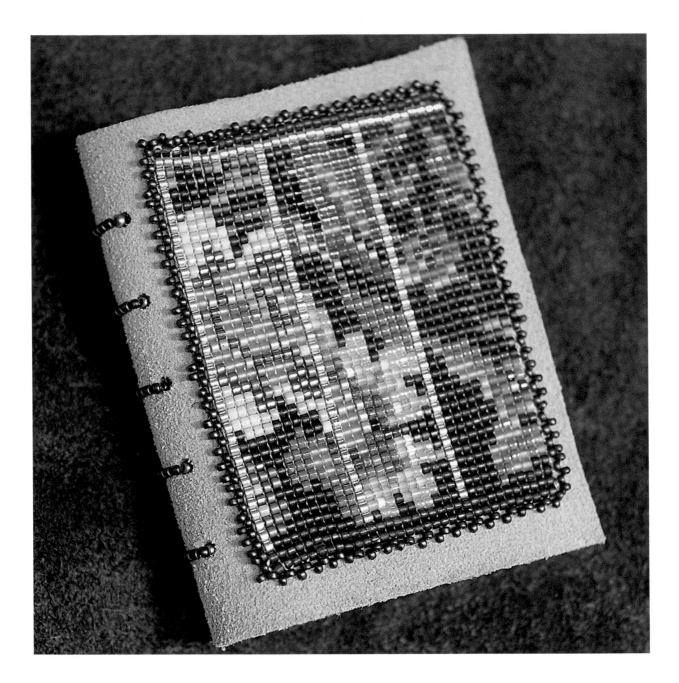

Floral Medley
Needle Book

Like the previous project using the thread spool, this needle book uses portions of a larger graph. In this case, however, I have taken small sections of the large floral design #H08 (page 34) and worked them side-by-side, separated by a single gold bead. The result is a different effect of a nice collage of floral patterns similar to patchwork designs.

Finished size closed book:
2½" wide x 3¼" tall.

Materials

- Size 11 Delica beads* as follows:
  - 2 grams purple/blue #377
  - 1 gram gold #041
  - 1 gram each yellow-green #371, #797, and #663
  - 1 gram each blue-green #373, #374, #859, and #327
  - 1 gram each yellow #623, #771, and #22L
  - 1 gram each peach #353, #207, #684, #564, and #703
  - 1 gram each pink #234, #678, #253, #281, and #296
  - 1 gram burgundy #611
  - 1 gram each purple #1347, #661, and #610
  - 1 gram each blue #078, #879, #862, and #693
- 2 grams* dark blue size 15 seed beads
- 5" x 3¼" leather piece, or ½" longer and twice as wide plus 1" of your finished beadwork design
- Leather hole punch for small holes, or X-acto knife
- 4¼" x 2⅞" blue felt piece
- 4¼" x 2⅞" purple felt piece
- Dark blue beading thread
- Beading needle
- Several Post-It Notes®
- Leather glue

*Bead amounts are approximate. You may need slightly more or less depending on your finished piece.

General Instructions

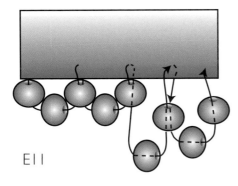

E11

1 Use the chart or choose a portion or portions of a design and frame them off with Post-It Notes. If using multiple sections of designs, make sure they are equal in length, unless you want to make the design longer in one section.

2 Stitch the beadwork. I made mine in loomwork, but you could use any stitch you choose that will work for a square or rectangular graph. If working the chart on facing page in herringbone stitch, omit the far right column.

3 Bead an edging around your finished piece using the size 15 beads. I used edging #E11, shown again at left.

4 To assemble the book, cut or punch pairs of holes in the leather, about ³⁄₁₆" apart from each other, and an equal distance from the center spine of the "book." Make each set of holes about ½" away from the top and bottom of the book and from each other.

5 Place the felt, centered, on the inside section of the leather and stitch through the holes of the spine of the book, catching the felt and stringing beads from one hole to the next on the outside of the book. Weave in ends.

6 Glue the beadwork to the front of the book and let dry.

Chart

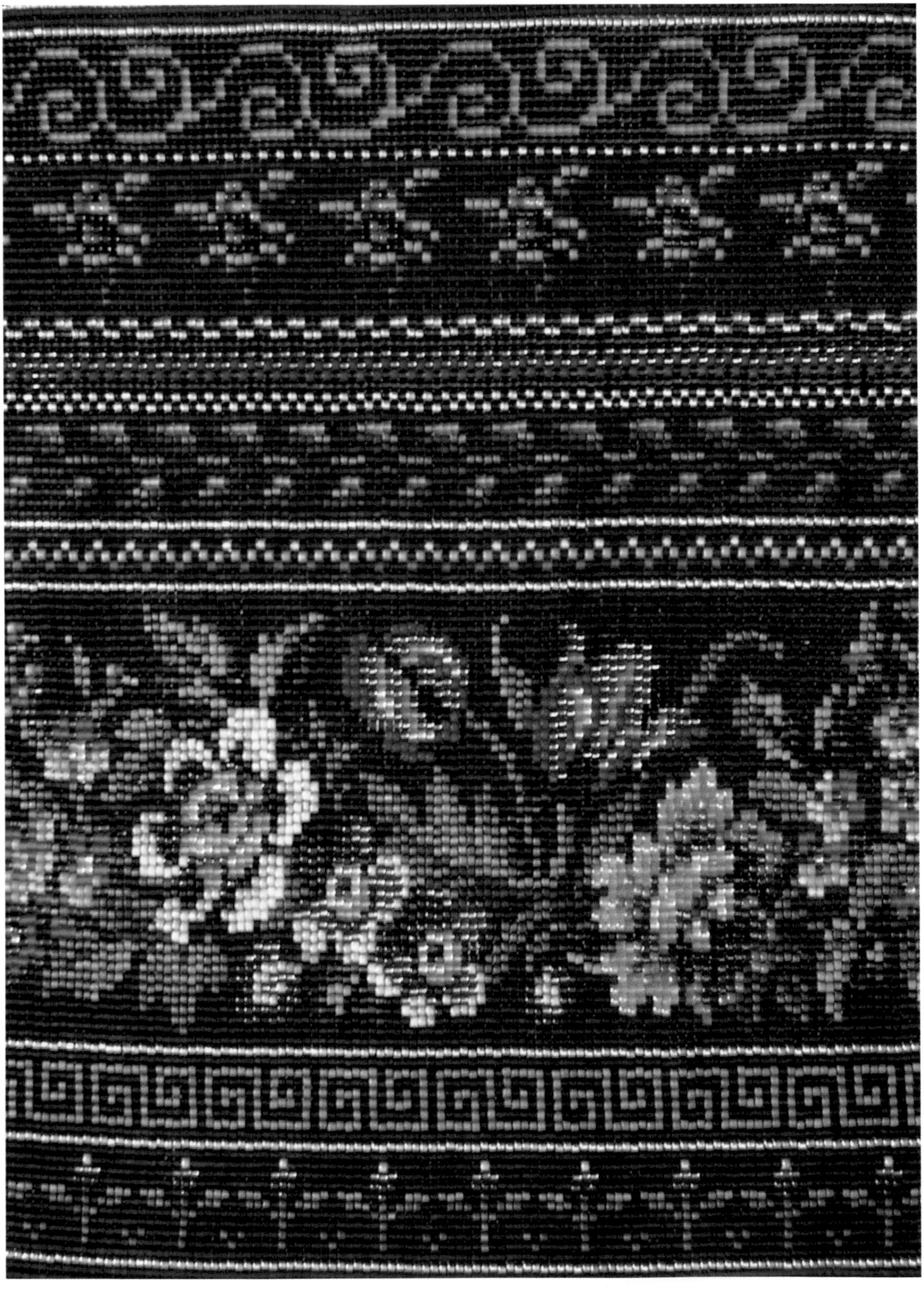

This is the project on the cover of the book. It shows how you can create a design by combining large and small patterns throughout the book to make one large composition. It also shows how you can use some of the graphs for other beadwork techniques, since the graph is for herringbone, yet I stitched the design on the loom. When planning this project, I started with the large floral, then, using colors from that pattern, added different repeating patterns from florals to abstracts, and separated each with a single strip of gold beads, or a small pattern of gold.

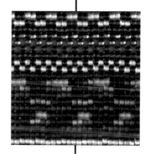

Loomwork Wall Hanging

Finished size of beadwork:
7¼" wide x 8½" tall.

Materials

- Size 11 Delica beads* as follows:
  - 30 grams purple/blue #377
  - 8 grams gold #041
  - 8 grams each yellow-green #371, #797, and #663
  - 8 grams each blue-green #373, #374, #859, and #327
  - 4 grams each yellow #623, #771, and #22L
  - 4 grams each peach #353, #207, #684, #564, and #703
  - 4 grams each pink #234, #678, #253, #281, and #296
  - 4 grams burgundy #611
  - 4 grams each purple #1347, #661, and #610
  - 4 grams each blue #078, #879, #862, and #693
- Bead loom that can work 134 beads across
- White beading thread
- Beading needle

*Bead amounts are approximate. You may need slightly more or less depending on your finished piece.

General Instructions

1 Warp the loom for 134 beads.

2 Work the pattern in the chart.

3 Weave in the ends and frame your picture.

Here is an example of picking and choosing charts and projects. This detail photo shows the large floral pattern from the Loomwork Wall Hanging project worked in herringbone stitch in size 15 beads in a variation of the Fleur-de-lis Gate Purse project that appears here.

Chart

Fleur-de-lis Gate Purse

This purse shows how you can use a fairly simple design, and then make the project very elaborate by adding a complex fringe. The fleur-de-lis pattern is #H01 (page 33). The fringe is in two layers around the bottom of the purse, with a single dangle in the middle. There are also small dangles added at the top of the purse.

Fleur-de-lis Gate Purse

Materials

Finished size, including fringe and frame:
2½" wide × 7" long (not including strap).

- Expandable gate type purse frame (expandable to about 2½")
- 75 grams* pink silver-lined size 11 seed beads
- 8 grams* burgundy size 11 seed beads
- 4 grams* size 6 pink silver-lined seed beads
- 4 grams* size 11 pink #256 Delica beads
- 4 grams* size 11 burgundy #12 Delica beads
- 4 grams* size 8 silver-colored seed beads
- 1 gram* size 15 burgundy seed beads
- 36 diamond-shaped garnet beads
- 17 polished garnet chips (for wrist strap)
- 65 burgundy teardrop beads
- 40 ⅛"-long silver bugle beads
- 129 ⅛"-long drop pearls
- 100 rose quartz chip beads
- 28 ⅛"-long pink faceted beads
- 1 pink butterfly bead
- 2 pink flower beads
- Beading needle
- Pale pink beading thread

*Bead amounts are approximate. You may need slightly more or less depending on your finished piece.

General Instructions

1 To make the circular netting and herringbone stitch bag, stitch the bottom netting following the instructions below, then add two pink size 11 seed beads between every three beads along the perimeter of the netting, including the center bead of each five bead set in row 17 as one of the beads on the last row.

Unless otherwise noted, each progressing row is worked only in the beads of the previous row.

Row 1: String three beads and tie a square knot.

Row 2: String two beads and pass through the next bead. Repeat around and pass through the first bead in the row.

Row 3: String one bead and pass through the next bead. Repeat around and pass through the first bead in the row.

Row 4: String two beads, pass through the next bead. Repeat around and pass through the first bead in the row.

Row 5: String one bead, pass through the next bead. Repeat around and pass through the first bead in the row.

Row 6: String one bead, pass through the next bead. Repeat around and pass through the first bead in the row.

Row 7: String three beads, pass through the next bead. Repeat around and pass through the first two beads in the row.

Row 8: String three beads, pass through the center bead of row 7's three-bead set. Repeat around and pass through the first bead in the row.

Row 9: String three beads, pass through the third bead in row 8's three-bead set and the center bead in row 7's three-bead set and the first bead in the next three-bead set of row 8. Repeat around and pass through the first two beads in the row.

Row 10: String 5 beads, pass through the center bead of row 9's three-bead set. Repeat around and pass through the first four beads in the row.

Row 11: String three beads and pass through the three center beads of row 10's five-bead set. Repeat around and pass through the first three beads of the row.

Row 12: String five beads and pass through three beads. Repeat around and pass through the first five beads in the row.

Row 13: String three beads and pass through five beads. Repeat around and pass through the first two beads in the row.

Row 14: String three beads, pass through the center bead of row 12's five-bead set. String three beads and pass through the center bead of row 13's three-bead set. Repeat around and pass through the first two beads in the row.

Row 15: String five beads and pass through the center bead of the three-bead set. Repeat around and pass through the first three beads in the row.

Row 16: String five beads and pass through the center bead of the five-bead set. Repeat around and pass through the first three beads in the row.

Rows 17 and 18: Repeat row 16.

2 Stitch another five rounds of herringbone stitch using the pink size 11 seed beads, and then begin the fleur-de-lis pattern in chart. (The chart shows just the patterned section.) Work the pink color in herringbone stitch for the remainder of each row.

3 After finishing the chart, work 20 more rounds of the pink background color.

(continued)

Note

The center bead in each bead loop of rows 12, 13, and 15 are the beads used for Fringes 1, 2, 3, and 4 on the bottom of the bag. One way to make it easy to find these beads when beading the fringe is to use a different-colored bead for the center bead on these rows. You only need a slightly different-colored pink bead, so you can easily find these beads when working the fringes.

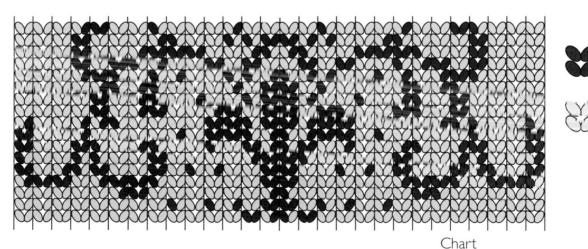

Chart

Legend

75 grams of pink silver-lined size 11 seed beads

8 grams of burgundy size 11 seed beads

4 grams of size 6 pink silver-lined seed beads

4 grams of size 11 pink Delica beads #256

4 grams of size 11 burgundy Delica beads #12

4 grams of size 8 silver-colored seed beads

1 gram of size 15 burgundy seed beads

36 diamond-shaped garnet beads

17 polished garnet chips (for the wrist strap)

65 burgundy teardrop beads

40 1/8"-long silver bugle beads

129 1/8"-long drop pearls

100 rose quartz chip beads

28 1/8"-long pink faceted beads

1 pink butterfly bead

2 pink flower beads

To attach beaded bag to gate frame:

1 Pass through six beads of the last round, string a pink size 11 seed bead, pass through a hole in the gate frame, and then pass back through the bead strung, as shown in Figure 1. Repeat around the purse. For strength, pass through the beads and frame holes again.

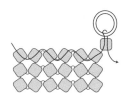

Figure 1

2 For the fringe along the gate frame, string through the top row of beads, adding the dangle in Figure 2, halfway between each set of six beads between each frame hole.

Figure 2

To complete the bottom fringe:

The fringe at the bottom of the bag is worked from the outer fringes in burgundy (Fringe 1 and 2), to the inner pink fringes (Fringe 3 and 4), to the center dangle on the middle bottom of the bag.

1 For Fringe 1 and 2, follow the pattern in Figure 3, passing through the center bead on row 15 on the bottom netting of the bag, then stringing the Fringe 1 pattern, then skipping five five-bead sets on row 15 and passing through the center bead on the next five-bead set on row 15. Repeat until you have worked four repeats around the bag, and are at the beginning of the first repeat.

2 Pass through the beads on the bottom of the bag until the thread is coming out of the center bead of the five-bead set on row 15, halfway between Fringe 1. Begin Fringe 2 here, working in the same manner as you worked Fringe 1.

3 For Fringe 3 and 4, follow the pattern in Figure 4, passing through every-other center bead of rows 12 and 13 on the bottom netting of the bag, and stringing the fringe pattern (Fringe 3 and 4 are the same) between each center bead. When you get all the way around once, you will be coming out of a bead that is halfway between the first dangle, and you will have finished Fringe 3.

4 Begin Fringe 4 by repeating the process worked for Fringe 3, passing through each bead halfway between Fringe 3's dangles.

5 For the center dangle, follow the pattern in Figure 5, passing through the three beads in row 1 of the bottom of the bag. Weave in ends.

(continued)

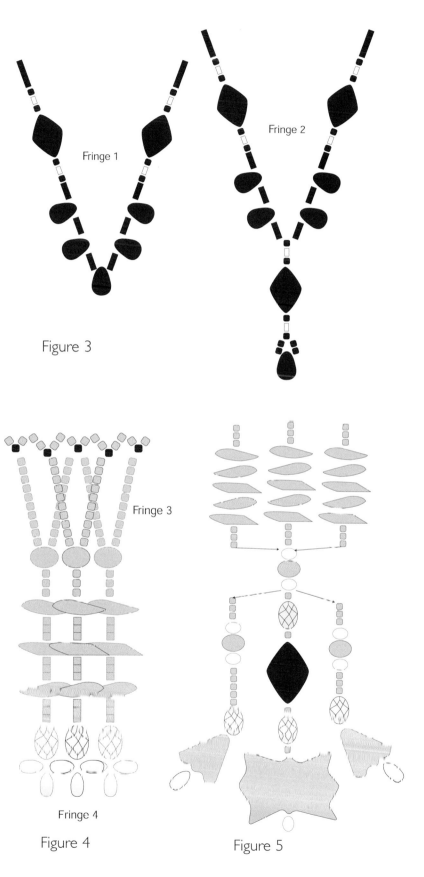

Figure 3

Fringe 1

Fringe 2

Fringe 3

Fringe 4

Figure 4

Figure 5

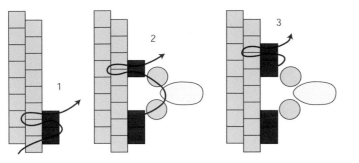

Figure 6

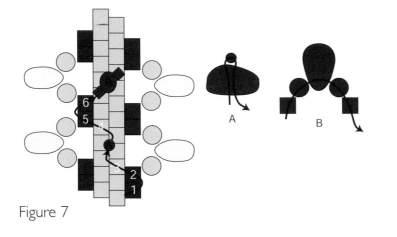

Figure 7

A

B

For the wrist strap:

The wrist strap is a simple peyote stitch strip embellished on the sides and top with a variety of beads.

1 Make a two-bead-wide peyote stitch strip, 128 pink Delica beads long, or to the desired length in repeats of four beads.

2 Add the side edging to the strap, following the three steps shown in Figure 6. Repeat steps 2 and 3 of Figure 6 to the end of the strap. Repeat on the other side of the strap.

3 To make the bead detail on the top of the strap, pass through beads 1, 2, and 3 shown in Figure 7. String one garnet and one size 15 seed bead, as shown in "A" on Figure 7, and then pass through beads 4, 5, and 6.

4 String the pattern shown in "B" on Figure 7, then repeat to the end of the strap.

5 Stitch the strap to the loops on the purse frame, passing through the loops and the end of the strap several times for strength. Weave in ends.

Contributing Artists

The gallery photos throughout this book showcase pieces created by some very talented artists. The following are brief biographies for those wonderful beaders.

Margo C. Field

Margo "discovered" beads in 1990. After retiring from a career in Hospital Pharmacy, she opened Poppy Field Bead Company in Albuquerque, New Mexico. She teaches many classes at her store and workshops across the United States.

Store address: Poppy Field Bead Company

2531 Jefferson NE Suite 140

Albuquerque, New Mexico 87110

Phone: (505) 880-8697

E-mail: beadfield@poppyfield.com

Web site: www.poppyfield.com

Kathy Henjyoji

Kathy is a self-taught designer and a teacher. Beading compliments her many artistic interests, which include dancing, music, and theater. She enjoys the diversity of beading displayed in her uniquely designed jewelry, ranging from eclectic to traditional. Kathy often will combine and interchange several techniques within one piece.

Corinne Loomer

Corinne designs and teaches needlework in a variety of media. She enjoys quilting, crocheting, knitting, designing jewelry, and working with polymer clay. Corinne's curiosity of new techniques and her commitment to mastering her art will inspire you.

Liz Smith

Liz teaches beading classes at Creative Castle in Newbury Park, California, and at San Gabriel Bead Co in San Gabriel, California. She is represented at The Artist Studio in Palos Verdes, California. Liz says: "Beads have taken over a major portion of my time, and I enjoy working with the incredible

palette of color, shapes, and textures. I am drawn to the luster and sparkle of these incredible bits of glass. I relish the freedom of starting with a simple idea and the excitement of letting the beads dictate the shape and form of the finished piece. I love creating a piece that causes people to stop, stare, to reach out, and want to touch."

Lisa Taylor

Lisa's jewelry designs are enhanced and embellished by her passion for beading. Color and texture are paramount to the design of each unique creation. Her vast knowledge, experience, and more than 10 years of study in color theory truly bring life, voice, and enchantment to her one-of-a-kind works. Lisa's needle artistic expressions include needlepoint, embroidery, tatting, quilting, knitting, and traditional rug hooking. Lisa's designs are offered in Beverly Hills, California, and are available on consignment. Her credits include designing for celebrities, and being featured in various books and exclusive items showcased on television.

Carole Tripp

Carole has had her designs published in several books. She teaches beading classes and is an avid promoter of beadwork, hosting biweekly bead get-togethers at her store, Creative Castle in Newbury Park, California. When not beading, Carole enjoys all types of needlework, softball, and spending time with her family.

Delinda Vannebrightyn Amura

Delinda is a nationally known instructor whose work is shown in galleries and museum collections, including several pieces in the beadwork collection at the Smithsonian. She strives to incorporate antique techniques, workmanship, and materials into her intricate designs.

General Index

Photos courtesy Margo C. Field

"Vineyard Version" by Margo C. Field.

Stitch Index

Bead Crochet Charts 71-77
Brick Stitch Charts 14-32
Buttonhole Stitch Charts 76-77
Edging Descriptions 90-93
Fringe Descriptions 94-98

Herringbone Stitch Charts 33-40
Loomwork Charts 41-49
Netting Charts 50-58
Peyote Stitch Charts 14-32
Square Stitch Charts 41-49

Chart Subject Index

Abstracts
  B11-B14, 16-17
  B19-B27, 18-20
  C03-C07, 71-72
  C13, 73
  C14, 73
  C19-C24, 74-76
  C29, 77
  C30, 77
  H01, 33
  H06, 33
  H07, 33
  H11, 35
  H12, 35
  H21-H26, 39-40
  L12-L13, 44
  L18-L28, 46-49
  N05, 51
  N06, 52
  N24, 56
  N26-N31, 56-58
Art Deco
  B28, 21
  B29, 22
Celtic Knots and Spirals
  B15-B18, 17-18
  B30, 22
  B31, 22
  C08-C12, 72-73
  C15-C18, 73-74
  H03, 33
  H04, 33
  L14-L17, 44-45
  L31, 49

L32, 49
N01-N04, 50-51
N08-N11, 52-53
N18-N21, 54-55
Dragons
  B27, 20
  L30, 22
Flowers
  B01-B04, 14
  B32-B37, 23-28
  C01, 71
  C27, 77
  C28, 77
  H02, 33
  H05, 33
  H08, 34
  H13, 36
  H15-H17, 37-38
  L01-L04, 41-42
  L11, 44
  L29, 49
  L30, 49

N07, 52
N12-N17, 53-54
N22, 55
N23, 56
N25, 56
Landscapes
  B38, 29
  B39, 30
Leaves
  B05-B10, 15-16
  B40, 31
  B41, 32
  C02, 71
  C25, 76
  C26, 77
  H09, 35
  H14, 36
  H18-H20, 38
  L05-L10, 42-43
Ocean
  H10, 35

"Clover Supplement" by Margo C. Field.

Photos courtesy Margo C. Field

Create Even More Beautiful Accessories

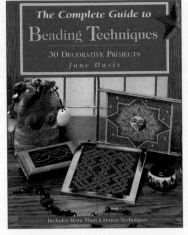
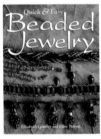
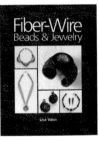